Un_bridled_
........conversations

Un*bridled*
........conversations

by Jonathan Bell

Forward by
Rhonda & James Tomasi

Unbridled Word Works
Hayden, Idaho
www.unbridledwordworks.com
info@unbridledwordworks.com

The conversations and events in this book are true or based on true conversations and events unless otherwise indicated. Some of the people and dialogues are blends or composites. The dialogues have been condensed for readability. Some names have been changed to protect the privacy of the people involved.

Published by **Unbridled Word Works**
P.O. Box 1301
Hayden, ID 83835
www.unbridledwordworks.com

Cover & book design by Nancy G. Daniel

ISBN 978-0-9793675-0-2

Printed in the United States of America
2007 - First Edition

GOD IS GOD.

He is Who He is.

*He is for Himself, accountable to
no doctrine, formula, system or theology.*

He does what He pleases and answers to no one.

He is God Almighty.

He is *eternally*
I AM.

Forward

IT IS NOT often that you meet a man of integrity, Godly character and faith; a man who truly stands in the face of adversity and accepts the consequences with grace and humility. Finding a man you truly respect, even though there is sometimes a conflict of viewpoints, is comforting. You know you can depend on him to be truthful to the tenacious grip of God on his life. We look for that person who will express what he believes in an uncompromising stand for what is right and just, although sometimes unpopular in man's opinion, while risking judgment and misunderstandings. Jonathan is such a man.

Jonathan Bell earned our respect when we first met in Coeur d'Alene, Idaho. Over the years since, we've watched him follow God as a *hart that pants after the water brooks*. He is candid about his failures and undeniably a slave to his Lord, Jesus.

It has been our pleasure to share with him in intimate conversations about God's kingdom. We've found it interesting that his *Unbridled Conversations* with God align so well with true kingdom mentality, a mentality that so few have embraced or understand. His writings unabashedly embrace and allude to questions we've all had on this walk. He openly connects his life to our own in the subtlety of hidden remorse over the rejection of God in our modern churches, while offering the Lord's loving response to abuses and oversights regarding those in the kingdom who have a heart to follow God with all their mind, soul and strength.

This book is a must-read for those who have encountered devastating news, faced pain, lived with discouraging thoughts of hopelessness and faced situations they believed were their demise. Jonathan portrays the love God has for us, while encouraging us to p*ress on* and live by His grace—not by our interpretation of life's disastrous circumstances. We encourage readers to share the truth encapsulated in this book with friends and family.

James & Rhonda Tomasi
Upper Cervical Advocates in Marketplace ministry
www.whattimetuesday.com, www.icservants.org

Preface

PEOPLE HAVE TOLD me that I say things that others won't say. A delightful, elderly lady once said, "You say the things that we're afraid to say, things that we're not sure are okay."

Is that true? In a world where everything is fair game to criticize, defame, exaggerate, insult or claim, are Christians partly excluded from free speech? Do we feel that some things are not "okay" to say? We joke about political correctness, but are we guilty of religious correctness? I'm not a big proponent of free speech. Though I did my time as somewhat of a radical, I'm pretty conservative politically and in lifestyle. I served in the army, I know how to set a proper table, I like opening doors for women, and I believe some things should be off-limits. But, as Christians, we should have the least to fear from our spiritual brothers and sisters if we ask basic questions about our faith. We should feel free to converse and to express our doubts, questions and fears without being subjected to condemnation or ridicule.

God has spoken to me many times, in many ways, about many things, and I believe he has asked me to write about some of my experiences. This is not intended to be about me in an autobiographical sense, nor is it intended to be an occasion for ax grinding. Though axes to grind are available, I hope to avoid the temptation. Since it is difficult to write about such experiences without including some biography, I have placed my conversations with God and others in the context of my life. They make more sense that way.

It will be obvious that the five years preceding this writing have been years of personal confusion. Hopefully the confusion will be obvious in the dialogues and observations, but not so much as to make them unreadable. I have aimed for a balance between clarity and chaos. And the chronology of the events surrounding the conversations is less important than the content and implications of the dialogues.

I would like to dedicate this to people who have unanswered basic questions, whose pain is misunderstood, who feel inferior to the great talents exhibited in their churches, who inhabit the edges of the Christian experience, and especially to all those who feel as if they fell off the Christian train somewhere and are staring down empty tracks.

If a major part of our purpose as believers is to reveal God to unbelievers, I hope to reveal something of an unbelievable God to believers.

And, finally, if what is conveyed here causes an enlargement of thinking and understanding of God, then my purpose, which hopefully is His purpose, has been fulfilled.

Thanks to Rhonda and James Tomasi, who invited me into their home, while I wrote. Thanks especially to Sherron Walstad for her substantial critical and editorial input. Her sensitivity and kind suggestions were essential in helping me sort through what I should and should not say. Their support and the encouragement of others have been invaluable.

But then, I've had a lot of help. That's part of the story.

Prologue

God loves everyone. He is love. His nature is to love. I'm sure of it. I often wonder, though, does He *like* everyone?

I HAVE FASHIONED an imaginary friend I'll call "Brad" as a composite of many people I have met, with whom I never quite see eye to eye. Talking with Brad is somewhat like a conversation over an intermittent cell phone connection so common in the rural Northwest where I've spent most of my adult life. At times, I'm unsure that what I've said was heard or that I've heard what was said by the other person. Brad showed up often.

"Hey, Jonathan!"

"Hey, Brad. What's up?"

"Not much. What'er you up to?"

"Writing a book."

"Really?"

"Yep. I believe that the Lord told me to write a book."

"You know what, buddy?"

"What?"

"I believe it. But I thought you were an engineer. You know, machines and stuff. You're a hardware guy. Can you write a book?"

"Well, maybe. Perhaps it'll have to be published in hardcover only."

"That's pretty bad, man. I would leave that out."

"I'll think about it."

"You know, I can see you writing a book. Just when you said that, I got a good feeling, like a witness or something."

"Cool. So you like the idea?"

"I do. If you can put a machine idea together, a book should be simple. Just try to keep it acceptable, okay?"

"We can't always be acceptable. I believe the Lord wants me to write some things down just the way I've experienced them."

"Well, hey, you just tell it like you see it. You know? Just be honest and tell it straight."

"I'll try. Hey, you're going to be in it, bro."

"I am?"

"Yep. You will be one of the main characters, though you're really a

1

composite of a lot of people like you."

"Me? A composite? I don't feel like a composite."

"You will when I'm done, believe me, and I'm going to try to get as many of our conversations in as I can."

"I don't know. That's a lot of stuff, man. I mean, we've covered a lot of ground in all the years I've known you. How long *have* I known you?"

"Seems like all my life, Brad. Seems like all my life."

"So what are you going to say about me?"

"Not a lot about you personally, just as much of the stuff that we've disagreed on as I can remember."

"What? Why just our disagreements? We've shared a lot of stuff that we both agree on. You know that."

"You're right, but people aren't interested in agreement. They want to read about conflict and tension. How would you feel if you went to a movie and all the actors just sat around having a good time, agreeing with each other?"

"Cheated, I guess."

"Exactly."

"Well, it's a good thing that I've won most of our arguments, or I'd look bad."

"Good point. But remember, I still get to choose which arguments I'll write about."

"Yeah, but then it could be one-sided in your favor."

"My book, Brad."

"Okay, okay. Anyway, I'm looking forward to reading about my sound advice. Except, don't put any jokes in it, okay? Especially the suicide joke."

"Come on, Brad, trust me. Would I do that?"

"Trust you? I trust you to be you. Yeah, remember when you said that …?"

"Hold on. You're jumping the gun. I need to work up to that."

"Yeah, okay. Hey, I'm on a mission today. Gotta go. Be seeing ya."

"You bet. See ya, Brad."

1

Conversations

Talk may be cheap, but good conversation should be highly valued.

IF I WERE asked what the enjoyable things in life are, while perhaps not the first thing, conversations would certainly be up there close to the top. Someone once remarked somewhere that the shortest distance between two destinations is good company, implying good conversation.

Eating and sex are certainly frontrunners for enjoyment, and a good night's sleep is high on the scale. Personally, I like some adrenaline activities like dirt biking and snowmobiling. Mixing it up with a few buddies on some high-performance toys can be a blast. For relaxing, sitting by a campfire, listening to and telling stories can be hard to beat, though an intimate dinner at a cozy restaurant with someone special might top that. Most of the good things in life involve others and interacting with them in different ways. The most common way is through conversation.

Some people are gifted conversationalists, easily able to bring a natural balance to the dialogue arena, which creates an atmosphere of ease and pleasantness. *You're a good listener*, are words we like to hear. It's a compliment implying selflessness and a quiet spirit. But conversing is more than just listening. Listening only is somewhat of a cop-out. Sometimes we can be there simply for someone to unload on, which is okay, as there's a place for that. But that isn't true conversation. Though it is often appropriate to just listen, sometimes we fail to speak out when we should.

Conversing requires a fairly even mix of listening and speaking, along with suitable body language like positioning and eye contact. The even mix does not necessarily have to take place in each segment of the conversation. Good conversation among people who interact often can take place over a long period of time, with one person playing the listener for a while and then the roles reversing. I don't claim to be a good conversationalist. In fact, I have been lousy, but I'm making progress as I discover the value, pleasure and intimacy of deep dialogue.

Rather than *you are a good listener*, let *you are a good conversationalist* be heard. And as God speaks to us through diverse means, a response is expected which can be prayer. I have some limited ability to comprehend prayer, but God wants us to pray.

Though discretion is required, we should be more outspoken. Saying out loud or writing our thoughts clarifies our position, and doing so can be beneficial or harmful. Once said or written, those words cannot be retrieved. They are out there, for good or for ill. That's the danger and power of words.

But as a man, I like danger and power.

I GREW UP just north of Baltimore, a sort of secondary city, a working town, once known for its harbor's easy access to the famed Chesapeake Bay, land of pleasant living—or so I heard as a child. Though large areas of Baltimore have since been transformed, much of the local industry deteriorated as I was gaining years. The once-thriving docks were reduced to vacant warehouses, rusting railroad tracks and dark back alleys frequented by a culture I remained safe from in my middle-class neighborhood. I didn't actually hang within the city too much, though I played some piano with a local band around the area. Occasionally I had thoughts of being a musician someday, but my father eventually decided otherwise.

"You know that band you play in?" he asked, when I was about fourteen.

"Yeah, sure," I answered. "Pretty great, huh?"

"You're not in it anymore."

"Oh, you're wrong. They like me just fine. I don't know where you heard that."

"No. *I* said you're not in it anymore," he informed me. "You're going to study hard and be an engineer. Forget about music. It's over."

It was disappointing, but it was wisdom. The band guys were quite a lot older and probably not a good influence, considering the occasional drinking and very late nights. Engineering was obviously a better plan. That the band went on to record a couple of successful records only bothered me for a few years. No big deal.

I recall feeling lonely. As a distraction from my loneliness, I frequently built and tested mechanical devices in our basement. My occasional backyard, home-made rocket launches probably caused our neighbors some tension. As for music, I had taken one piano lesson. The teacher suggested football as being more appropriate. Football? No good. Too confusing. All those rules and regulations to follow? Next, since I was tall, I had been lured into basketball. Tell me once more, which way is our goal or basket? Lacrosse was a worse nightmare, with people running in all directions. The only sport I could make sense of was wrestling, where I could get hold of something and work on it— well, actually a person—by myself. I haven't changed much in many ways. As for the piano, I'd gotten a hold of that too. I played for hours to fill the time.

THE SUN TRULY rose in my life in the form of a blonde, silky-haired lady named Cathie who wandered into a record store I owned in Baltimore in February 1973. The store, where New Age music was sold, was my attempt to find an alternative to progressing through the ranks from basic engineer to high management at Black and Decker Manufacturing Company, where my real job was. Cathie said she lived upstairs and that she was the one who had called down for a song request perhaps a week earlier. A few of us played music around a Hammond B3 organ I had set up in the rear of the store, where I lived at the time. When she suggested a Coke or something, I was smitten.

Wow! Unlike the spacey, somewhat sullen and earthy types that frequented my life, Cathie was usually smiling and pleasant, wore a little makeup, and she obviously enjoyed life. And unlike me who tended to start off with the assumption that people didn't like me and then worked backwards from there, Cathie assumed acceptance and sort of dragged me into her lively realm. Man, she was fun!

No wonder. After meeting her mother and grandmother, who lived together in Florida, it was obvious that growing up in a warm, loving environment can radically alter your attitude toward others. Within a few months, I quit Black and Decker, closed the store, and Cathie and I drove around the country in a van we converted for light living. We eventually ended up near Kooskia, a small town in the north-central part of Idaho. We were married and began raising two children, Anna and Jonna. Cathie's mother and grandmother joined us, and I was delighted to have a close family. I felt loved and accepted. Finally, loneliness, my constant enemy, had been defeated, vanquished to haunt someone else, someone who had no one.

There were no companies near Kooskia looking to staff their engineering departments, so I turned to logging for a living. With a friend, I cobbled together something resembling a crane, attached it to a truck and managed to convince a charitable landowner to pay me to haul his logs to the mill. The contraption was very dangerous. Another charitable local suggested getting a real log loading/hauling outfit, and a local banker extended some financial mercy. Though I had never previously laid eyes on a chainsaw, much less a log-hauling truck, I managed to eventually become a bona fide logging contractor. You boys who like big toys should try running some seriously industrial logging machinery for a rush.

God was watching over me, even then. He had to be.

OUR MARRIED LIFE was made richer with an assortment of animals. Cathie collected animals the way some women collect figurines, though she did some of that too. Besides the traditional dogs and a cat or two, she added goats, horses, ground squirrels, a tree squirrel, ducks, swans, a raven, and probably some others to the mix.

For example, one day she decided she wanted a magpie, so I went down to the Salmon River, found a magpie nursery, climbed up a thorny tree—magpies are smart; they nest in the thorniest trees—grabbed a baby, and, trying not to bleed too much in the car, drove quickly back to our house and gave it to her. She was going to attempt to teach it to converse, sort of, but it soon fell into disfavor. We discovered its ability to transform, within a very short time, anything placed in its mouth into a puddle of gray-green goop. Cathie thought it was way too messy. I was intrigued, though, and amused myself trying foods of different textures and colors. They all came out the same. Impressive device, I thought. A real wonder of nature here, though even that became boring.

The magpie had to go, so I re-climbed the tree, replaced the baby bird, climbed down and waited, with fresh cuts, to see if the mother would accept it. I had heard that in the wild mothers don't accept returned offspring. However, the mother, after sufficiently scolding me, although I was simply trying to undo a wrong, returned to her nest and began feeding almost immediately. Good deal. No harm done to the bird, and I would heal quickly. While driving back home, I thought about what the bottom floor of the nest probably looked like. Baby birds were never again quite as cute.

Though I avoided much caretaking, which Cathie enjoyed, I liked the company of our animals and used to attach personalities to them and, therefore, conversations. Our dogs were a favored target. Once, when we needed a dog replacement, Cathie brought home Bruce. Though I like most dogs, and I liked Bruce, it was obvious that he was not a good fit. Too hyper for our local gang. Not our type. Nothing against pedigree if you have it, but we preferred blue-collar, working dogs with a somewhat quieter disposition. It was also clear that Tillie, our then-present dog, was not pleased with Bruce, nor were some of the other animals, in my opinion. I could easily imagine Tillie's plotting to get rid of Bruce.

"Hey, Bruce?"
"Yeah, Tillie?"
"You want to really make it with the owners?"
"Yeah, you bet. Make it with the owners."
"Catch the rooster."
"What? You serious?"
"Yep. Absolutely."
"What's a rooster?"
"See those birds over there?"
"Yeah, stupid birds."
"Well, the rooster is the odd-looking one. You can see that his tail is too big, and he occasionally chases the others, which is annoying to the humans. Catch him and you score big."
"Thanks, Tillie. I appreciate the suggestion. You know, I didn't think you liked me."

"I'm watching out for you, buddy. Go for it."

Bruce wasted no time. When Cathie came outside and found her bantam rooster's tail feathers in Bruce's mouth, she was anything but pleased. Now, I'm surprised that Bruce even got that close. Besides having the advantage of wings, in a race around a tight zigzag course where a rabbit would excel, a bantam rooster can hold its own. So Bruce was out, on to another owner. The rooster looked funny without tail feathers, which took a long time to grow back. I enjoyed watching him run around. It reminded me of a time when I'd lost my tail feathers, but they eventually grew back too. Life was all right.

I HAVE HAD conversations with God. Whether or not God speaks to us or whether or not it was God who was speaking to me could be questioned, but I'm not going to attempt to present evidence that it was God. A few of the conversations may convince some that the One who seems to be speaking couldn't be God because of the subject matter or the implications. That's the point. The One that I have assumed is God may not come in an acceptable form. I am presenting God as I have experienced Him, One who knows no bounds, a Being unacceptable to some, perhaps.

I have been taught many things in church, in Bible studies, from reading books, from TV, teaching cassettes and CDs. Though it may not be evident, I have spent considerable time studying the Bible. I've listened to the doctrines of many different denominations and tried to keep abreast of the latest trends in spiritual "revelation." I certainly haven't heard everything. However, the One I know as God has quite often presented Himself as many times larger and, at least, much less predictable than the one usually presented to me by others.

Some of what God has said to me can be written down verbatim, and there is no room for embellishment or paraphrasing. I believe that the exact words are significant and should be presented precisely. Though I may add an interpretation, I make no claim as to its being the correct or only interpretation. The reader may interpret the words differently. Are these words a conversation? I believe so, because, while not immediate, there is a response of some kind required either to Him or to others. Though a particular experience of His speaking directly may be one-sided, presenting the words to others results in interesting responses.

When the Lord first began speaking to me, it was not immediately apparent that He wanted me to convey to others what He said. I should have assumed He would, at least eventually, want others to hear these things. I view some of His speaking to me as if He starts with a sort of template and then fills in various parts over time to form a reasonably complete concept. So some things make more sense now that time has passed.

There are times when the conversation is an interaction of thoughts. Though I'm sure it is God who is speaking to me, I have to convert those thoughts into word format. There is room for error, but I believe the essence of the conversation is not difficult to convey. These conversations are the most enjoyable because there is room for some literary license in the conversion. The encounters are often startling, even alarming, and like a near miss with catastrophe, humor is occasionally found somewhere.

Along with the thoughts transfer, there is attitude or personality implied on both sides of the conversations, which I attempt to convey in the conversion. God has a lot of attitude and personality. He reigns supreme there. And I am fairly sure of the interpretation, since there is usually a direct application in my life. There are implied principles, though, which hopefully have some value to others. These principles may have significance on different levels for different people at different times. I also intend to make it apparent that, to me, God sort of makes it up as He goes along; that is, what He says or does one time may not apply the next time. Though He remains the same, Variety should certainly be one of His names.

Are people at different levels? I believe that there is a spiritual maturing process and that the same words can have different and/or deeper meaning to some. I'll leave it at that for the present, because some conversations address the subject of maturity.

God speaks to all of us through other people. Though the conversations with people actually took place somewhere and at some time, I have taken a lot of liberty to paraphrase and condense what was actually said. I have combined different conversations to distill the essence into various themes, which, hopefully, also display personalities and the uniqueness of our Christian lives. The characters I have fashioned are composites, and like Brad's name, their names are fictitious except where the conversation is truly original.

Many conversations were too intimate or personal to discuss, though the lessons were huge. As much as seems appropriate, I have incorporated these often tender and painful experiences into relatable dialogue. Real people have said these things, bared their hearts and souls, and God loves them all.

While the Lord has given me some information through dreams and visions, I have limited addressing much of that. I am still unsure of some interpretations, and there is little to relate as conversation.

Finally, there is inspiration—or divinely acquired knowledge, for one definition. Though I make conclusions which are drawn from a mix of the conversations and knowledge acquired from study or inspiration, the purpose here is not to present my doctrines or particular views on accepted teachings. Some commenting has been presented as dialogue because there is more than one legitimate argument. Perhaps additional meaningful debate will emerge.

2

Guidance

The straight and narrow path is not a single path that few of us find and walk on together. It is a path that each of us walks alone. Though straight in an inwardly spiritual sense, viewed from the outside, it may go all over the place.

IT WAS PROBABLY sometime in 1978, about a year after a friend led me in prayer and I committed my life to God, that I was sitting on my bed reading my Bible. The following scripture verse appeared to levitate off the page:

> I will instruct you and teach you in the way which you should go;
> I will counsel you with My eye upon you.
> Do not be as the horse or as the mule which have no understanding,
> Whose trappings include bit and bridle to hold them in check,
> Otherwise they will not come near to you. (Psalms 32:8–9)

So began my first long-running conversation with God. In the beginning I had no idea what this scripture implied. I was more amused that God was obviously drawing my attention to the words. I disagree with assuming that a particular scripture can be applied to someone's life as a personal promise or for personal direction without guidance from the Holy Spirit. God treats us all differently and it is unwise to make assumptions about what He might do. This time, though, I felt that God *was* speaking to me personally, and this particular scripture was the way it would be. At the time, I had no concept of the implications.

How could God counsel someone simply by watching them?

That God, Himself, would instruct me seemed implied at the time, but I dismissed it. After all, who was I that God would pay any particular attention to me?

Sometime later, just as I entered a Full Gospel Business Men's Fellowship International meeting, the leader walked over, introduced himself and said, "I see that you are one of God's special ones." *Special* ones? That was definitely worrisome.

It may seem nice to be special, but there are times when being special is not good. Few of us want to be singled out for special education. In the army, though I was a specialist, being otherwise special only meant trouble. In fact, I have always wanted simply to fit in. I was somewhat eccentric as a kid and not well liked by the cool guys I tried to hang with. College was extremely lonely since I had been rejected by the fraternities and had few friends.

On one hand, for those whose lives reflect success and security and have good social skills and experiences, being special might seem highly desirable. What could be so bad about being special? On the other hand, a lot of the special people in the Bible had difficult lives. It's interesting to read about their lives, but would we really want to live them? Would you like to dress in animal skins and subsist on a diet of locusts and wild honey? How about being swallowed by a fish, crucified, sawn in two or exiled to live alone on a remote island?

It could be assumed that such experiences are not part of today's Christianity. Few believe such things might actually happen. God wants to bless us and give us a comfortable life, right? Not necessarily. Bless us, yes. But blessings can come in unusual packages.

I HAD INTENDED to get my Christian education the normal way, by going to church, studying my Bible and trying my best to act and talk like a Christian. I signed on to be a follower of Jesus, skipped reading the fine print (I wouldn't have understood a word of it anyway), and figured that I could follow the rest of the followers as easily as I could follow Jesus. Stay with the crowd, was the plan. Don't stand out. After all, weren't we all headed down the same road together? The talk about how much God wanted to bless us sounded good to my ears.

Though some kind of subtle alarm sounded every time I heard the prosperity teaching that was popular at the time, I did not want to be in rebellion. Absolutely not. I was soon taught that rebellion was like witchcraft, something with which I wanted no part. I had found a group I could fit into, Jesus seemed to show up often, the Bible was very interesting, the music was good, and the Lord gave me a whole new way of looking at life.

A few weeks after my conversion, I woke up one morning literally loving God's creation, a new feeling which remained for a long time. Even my doubting wife, Cathie, couldn't ignore the changes and came on board within a couple of months. Still, another voice that seemed to want my attention was certainly present just outside my new Christian crowd.

But to fit in, I listened to the way others prayed and tried to structure my prayers the same way. "Oh, heavenly Father, thank You for blessing us and for this nice day and everything being so nice and all. Thank You for Your Son's dying for us and just loving us like You do, and for Your provision, the way You provide for us, and that You know all of our needs, and just meeting all our needs. Oh, Father, just bless our house and family and just all of those around us, and our church and all, and Father God, just bless those who just don't have a lot, and just be our Lord, and just be glorified in our lives, and just help us to just find Your perfect will, Father God, Jesus, and just love You, and just lift You up in our lives and just …"

"Would you get real here?"
"What?"
"Enough with all that. Tell me what's on your mind."

It was definitely a voice from above the ceiling. I was kneeling, elbows resting on what passed for a sofa in our partly remodeled, hundred-year-old house in Grangeville, Idaho, probably 1979.

"Do You really want to know what's on my mind?" I asked, somewhat in the form of a challenge, not entirely sure Whom I was addressing.

"Yes. Lay it all out for me just the way you feel about things," He said plainly.

I couldn't believe it. Lay it all out for Him? Tell Him what's on my mind? Who was this? It *had* to be Him. I had to think for a minute. Here was an open invitation to tell (apparently) God the truth. Did He actually want me to dump all of my fears, worries, anxieties and my anger on Him? Really? Did He want me to tell Him what I thought of how my life was going, what I really wanted and how frightened I was about the future? Was He interested in hearing how worried I was about providing for my young family and how concerned I was that I had made a fatal, unrecoverable error by not pursuing an engineering career? Did He want to hear it all? Everything? Why? Was He actually interested in my little life …? Maybe.

So I told Him every bit of it. I poured out every drop. I began a new way of talking to God, which I have maintained ever since. If that manner of talking straight, of taking every last feeling, problem, fear, frustration, hope, plan and failure to Him is not acceptable, it's too late now. Certainly there are times for formal prayer, for praise, for counting blessings and giving thanks. Structure should be significant in our prayer life, of course. But more important is the need to get real with Him and express things that we might be afraid of another's hearing, or even of His hearing (as if He had no idea already). Tell it all, and tell it straight. He knows what's inside us, and saying it out loud can bring healing.

I say that it *can* bring healing, though there is no guarantee that anything we may expect will result from our prayers. Really? We are taught to pray. We should pray, and though I've read books and heard countless sermons and teachings on prayer, prayer remains somewhat of a mystery, at least to me.

The Lord did admonish me early on to pray more consistently. He implied that I usually waited until I was in a tough spot, down in some crevice, before I got serious about praying. Though I could not avoid the "crevice" by going around, I could pray a sort of bridge over some obstacles if I would start praying sooner. It probably would have been a good idea to follow His suggestion, and I may have succeeded a few times. I don't know. I can't remember looking down into any crevice I avoided, though I *can* remember looking up a lot of times.

NOW, THE LORD had performed many supernatural works that I had personally witnessed. I observed instantaneous healings, miraculous provision, absolutely spot-on words of knowledge and foreknowledge.

Many times God intervened on behalf of others I knew. Therefore, when my wife was overdue with our second child, Jonna, I was convinced that He would take care of things. My faith was simply being stretched, I supposed.

However, when our exasperated doctor finally warned me that my wife's and unborn child's lives were in real danger, I agreed to a Caesarian section. Though it wouldn't be the first time, many of my full-of-faith friends were disappointed. To them, I was obviously lacking in faith. That may have been true, but as I sat in the waiting room I asked God a question.

"Why? You've done so many wonderful things. This is simple. Deliver the baby. Why not show us again how great You are?"

"I chose not to," was the almost audible reply.

God chose not to. He makes the choices. Faith is good. Believing is great. Confession is, well, fine. But He still makes the choices. *"I am sovereign, is the standard here,"* was quite clearly implied. *"Can you deal with that?"*

"I guess I will," I muttered. That's the way it would be, I would learn.

That experience was the first true example of what I began to see as an overriding sovereignty, which made all of the suppositions about promises from God open to speculation. Does God answer prayer? I believe that He hears our prayers, but I don't believe He promises anywhere to answer every one. Personally, I hope He has forgotten a few I've asked during some very frustrating times. Can we trust God to deliver on His promises? That depends on what has been promised to whom and when. In the epistle to the Hebrews we are reminded of a whole lot of people who apparently received nothing. I hear a lot of teaching about prayer which seems based on assumptions. More about that later.

AROUND 1980, I had a conversation with my older daughter. I had been born-again for about three years, and she was riding with me in my 1979 White Western Star log truck equipped with a hydraulic self-loader. It was a complex machine. I was easing my way down the road off of Mt. Idaho, south of Grangeville. She rocked forward slightly as I occasionally applied the brakes.

"Dad, what are you doing with your foot?" Anna asked.

"My foot? I'm braking a little now and then to keep our speed down. I'm using the brakes to slow the truck."

"Dad?"

"Yes, Anna."

"How do the brakes work?"

Anna, now four, had begun to ask difficult questions. It would have been easy to say, "Too complex for you to understand." But she was smiling at me, waiting for an answer. She deserved something. I wanted to satisfy her desire for information, but what could I say? How could I explain to a four-year-old how a truck's air brakes worked? I thought of an analogy.

"Well, you know your round bouncy horse?"

"Yeah."

"We use a bicycle pump to put air in it?"

"Yeah."

"You know that it gets bigger as we pump more air into it?"

"Yeah."

"Well, there is something like that bicycle pump under the front of this truck, but the truck does the pumping for me. And there is a thing like your horse close to each one of the wheels on the truck."

"Okay."

"When I push on this pedal, that tells the truck to pump air into one of the things like your horse, which makes it so big that it sort of rubs against the wheel. The rubbing makes the wheel harder to turn, making the truck go a bit slower. Does that make sense?"

"Sure. That makes sense. Hey, look, Dad! Did you just see that big, huge bird?"

"It was a giant. What kind was it?"

"I dunno. You know, I'm getting hungry."

"Ten more minutes and I'll drop you off at the house on the way to the mill."

Now, I'm sure she has forgotten the conversation, but suppose she hasn't? Not that she would do this, but just suppose she were, as an adult, to go to a truck dealer and ask them about the pump and the bouncy horse? How embarrassing would that be? She could conclude that I had lied to her all those years ago. Though she certainly has more sense than that, I don't know that *we* do. We talk about the things of God like they are absolute, when I believe that He is infinitely more complex than we can even begin to comprehend. Listening to a lot of preaching, one might think that some have Him pretty well figured out. I doubt it.

Could much of our knowledge be comparable to bouncy horses and bicycle pumps? Could a portion of what we hold as profoundly absolute be merely symbolic of much more complex concepts?

BUT BACK TO counseling me with His eye on me. I have considered that phrase many times, read commentaries, and asked others. I only know that it has become a standard for determining His will for my guidance. For me, Psalms 32:8 has meant simply, *"I'm watching you, over you, around you and in you. Whatever involves you will not escape my awareness. Go and make decisions. Use the knowledge you have and gain more. Combine your knowledge with your experience and grow in wisdom. Do what appears right to you, what you feel you must do, or your best guess. Don't pay too much attention to what others may think or say. I will teach you. You will not go without instruction. I do not desire to have to tell you what you must do. Listen to my Spirit who dwells in you. He will lead you."*

The Spirit led Jesus into the wilderness. What kind of wilderness might the same Spirit lead us into?

"Hello, Brad," I said.

"JB. What's up?"

"Not much. What's up with you?"

"Just the regular stuff. So what did you do before you came to Idaho?"

"I was an engineer for Black and Decker, and I owned a store in Baltimore that sold New Age music, a lot of Eastern religion stuff."

"You were into Eastern religions?"

"Yep. I've always been interested in anything spiritual, but mostly

I was just looking for God. I lived in an apartment in the rear of the store, which also had a room where we had meetings."

"Secret meetings?"

"No. We just sat around in circles and chanted and stuff."

"Anything happen?"

"Oh, there were a few strange incidents. But I eventually came to realize that it was mostly self-worship and not much else. I had some personal problems, fears and things, and that New Age stuff only made some things worse. It was a big show. One of the local leaders, supposedly an 'enlightened one,' was just a regular businessman in it for the lifestyle and a decent living. I was actually asked to teach a few classes on Zen."

"Did you do it?"

"Yep, but I didn't show up for the first class."

"How come?"

"Well, the first lesson was that there was no instructor. Zen is referred to as *that which cannot be taught*. No instructor, no teaching. Christianity is the same in some ways."

"This should be good. Now I suppose you're going to tell me that Jesus was a Zen master."

"Interesting thought, but no. I would never reduce Him in any way, especially to the level of a mere Zen master. But like Zen must be experienced, so must Christianity be experienced. However, some are reluctant to truly experience God, and I believe that you can learn only a limited amount from reading and listening."

"That's not true. Most Christian leaders encourage people to seek the Lord directly, and many do. We're not in the Dark Ages here."

"You're right. They do. Though it seems that they still want to manage the experience somehow, to keep it within certain parameters rather than let God manage the experience. For example, when I was in the first grade, we studied cows. At the time, there was a working dairy nearby. On a field trip there, I finally stood face to face with a living, breathing Guernsey bull. All the information placed in my six-year-old brain did not prepare me for an actual confrontation with a live bull. The effect was dramatic. I remember standing there, eyes wide open, nose crinkled and mouth gaping. I had not imagined what I was looking at. The reality was nothing like what I had expected. I don't know why I was so amazed, except that I remember being overtaken by the magnitude of the disparity between what I had learned in class and what I was experiencing. If a picture is worth a thousand words, experience trumps a million pictures."

"But we have direct experiences with God. You know that. We're not warming pews in dead churches. Our churches are full of life."

"True, but even as dramatic as the bull experience was, it was limited. There were bars between the bull and me. I still think that in some ways, we or our leaders consciously or unconsciously place bars between us and God. Perhaps we have an unusual experience, and we or they say, 'That wasn't God.'"

"I can see your point, but not every voice speaking is from God, and we are only being reasonably concerned about the security of the body. Who needs some loose cannon shooting heretical doctrines at impressionable members of their congregations? Wolves in sheep's clothing abound, brother. Somebody has to watch over the flock."

"There is some agreement there, but I still think more chaos would be better."

"Come on. You can't let just anything go on at church meetings. Paul insists upon order. That's pretty clear. And we all have a desire to avoid unpleasant experiences."

"But perhaps we ourselves have a sort of filter that limits our exposure to God to those things we are assured will be agreeable," I said.

"You're saying that if we disagree with something, we might justify disregarding it by concluding that it isn't of God?" Brad asked.

"Yes. Then that validates my Zen experiment," I replied.

"What do you mean?"

"My supposed 'students' apparently chose to dismiss me as too lazy, or whatever, to show up rather than to believe that I was really offering them the opportunity to learn something. Nothing that comes to us in life is experientially useless. Romans 8:28 assures us of that. Congregations would have richer experiences with God if pastors had more trust in God's ability to manage their experiences. God actually knows a lot about caring for His sheep."

"You mean that leaders should trust God more with their congregations by allowing more openness in meetings, more dialogue?"

"Yes. That's one way."

"But that involves risk. People may get upset and leave."

"Exercising faith always involves risk. Failure and loss are valuable experiences," I argued.

"But people like winners. Losing is not attractive."

"Why do you suppose people were attracted to Jesus?" I asked.

"They gathered around Him because of the miracles and His astounding wisdom."

"People still gather around the same things, except entertainment is big now, though I suppose Jesus was pretty entertaining. Eventually, though, Jesus challenged His followers, almost tried to run them off. He told them that, 'He who eats My flesh and drinks My blood abides in Me, and I in him.' After hearing those difficult words, most left. The thought of eating a man's flesh was abhorrent to a Jew. They were particular about even which animals could be eaten. That was a very hard thing for a Jew to hear," I said.

"Hard for anybody, but it almost sounds like some kind of gathering and sorting going on."

"That's an interesting thought, Brad. I think that's part of the process. Yeah, God gathers, then sorts through the bunch. Paul even talks about such a thing going on in 1 Corinthians 11:19, 'For there must also be factions among you, in order that those who are approved may have become evident among you.'"

"So there is a process of gathering, testing and sorting going on. We seem to concentrate on gathering, as if that were the goal, when the process of sorting may be more important. Kind of like many are *gathered,* but few are *sorted out*?" Brad asked.

"Many are called, but few are chosen. Exactly. I like your thinking, my friend. Sometimes you're pretty sharp."

"You could also color this the other way, bro, and it could be an excuse for rebellion. Maybe you're just against what's established, and you're the problem."

"Could be."

"You ever worry about that?"

"I worry about everything. If I could flip a switch and make everything acceptable, I would in a minute. But I believe I know His voice, and that's the clincher. He said His sheep know His voice, and another they will not follow. I have to go with this. To me, following His voice is all I really know."

"Something to think about."

"We'll talk some more."

"You bet. But what happened the next week?" Brad asked.

"The next week?"

"At the Zen class."

"I don't remember. I guess I showed up, but the students didn't."

"Suppose they found another instructor?"

"No. I don't think they really wanted to learn anything. Most of the people I hung with were just in it for the lifestyle. It was all intellectually stimulating, it made them feel good, the music was emotionally arousing, and they were around people they were comfortable with."

"Good thing we Christians are so different. We're serving the real God."

"Yeah. Good thing we're *so* different," I said.

"Maybe you should write a book called Zen and the Art of Christianity."

"You're missing it, buddy," I said, looking down.

"Why?"

"That's like an oxymoron."

"What?"

"Zen and art. Zen is about experience, and art is for display," I argued.

"Art is about expressing what's inside," Brad said.

"Hmm. Good thought, Brad. Doggone it. You amaze me at times. We could open up some interesting comparisons with commercial art …"

"Not going there now, bro. We'll be here forever."

"No problem. See ya."

"Yeah, later."

3

The Prayer

Into the darkest places I go that I may see the light.
Into the deepest depths I go that I may reach the height.
Beware the opposites, perceive the balance.
The wrong lies on either side of the right.

L ATE WINTER, 2001? It's hard to remember, but I was on my way
to work, driving north around Crays' corner on US Highway 95
between Grangeville and Cottonwood, Idaho. We called it Crays' corner,
because that's where the Crays lived.

I loved the Camas Prairie and life there. We knew so many people.
I had spent most of the previous twenty-five years in that area, starting out
as a logger, and then, since 1990, co-owning a successful manufacturing
business. I was an upper-medium size fish in a very small pond, which
suited me just perfectly. It was a fine pond to be swimming in.

It isn't easy to make a living in much of northern Idaho. There
was a time when hard work paid well. If you didn't own a ranch or a
farm, you could work in the woods or in the sawmills. Housing was not
high priced, and small-town America was alive and well long after it
had died in more accessible places.

When we arrived in 1973, Cathie and I had intended to do
the impossible, live off the land using horses and manual tools and
implements. I'm not sure why, and it was a dumb idea from the start.
Smarter people had long ago embraced technology and left the horse-
drawn implements rusting in the fields where they could be remembered
with dignity, having served intelligent people who mastered their use.
Being from the city, we supposedly had an edge over our less-well-

informed country brothers and sisters. So, with *Mother Earth News* in hand, we decided that we could defy human progress and prove that a superior lifestyle was possible there on Crane Hill, twelve miles east of Kooskia, Idaho.

The locals might have thought we were hippies, since I had the long hair and beard, but we liked bathing and good vehicles. Though I had a van, it was no microbus. It was a bought-new Chevy, three-quarter-ton, with a V8 and four-barrel. Sure, it was fixed up to live inside, but it had good radials and a limited-slip differential for an edge in bad weather. I probably would have installed a four-wheel-drive kit had they been available then.

No, I was into utility. I liked things to be useful. *Show* was not important. *Go* counted. When it appeared reasonably soon that living off the land was mainly for show, I turned to logging as a means to stay in Idaho, while others were leaving. I didn't like the hippies that much anyway. Unknown to me, a lot of our friends made their living growing and selling marijuana, and they questioned why I would make friends with the locals. I replied that the locals were fun, very sociable and, besides, I needed their help to make a living.

Around 1979, we upgraded from Kooskia, population eight hundred, to Grangeville, population thirty-five hundred, which was thirty miles to the south. I managed to make a living as an independent logging contractor and hauler until 1983, when I decided there was no more future in that line of work. No amount of hours or effort was enough to provide sufficiently. I was getting older and the timber industry was rapidly changing. I sold out and tried manufacturing and selling some products until, by 1986, all the money was gone. So, reluctantly, we left Idaho and moved in temporarily with my parents back in Baltimore.

I was employed near there until 1990. By then, we had accumulated enough money, mainly from the sale of our house which we had remodeled, to purchase half of a manufacturing business outside of good-old Grangeville. God brought us back to the place we loved. I never thought we would return, but He did it. We were home again.

Though once in a while, and increasingly more often, Psalms 106:15 came to mind, "And He gave them their request, but sent leanness into their soul," I was a busy man. Time was money. I had lost a lot of time, and I thought that by working hard enough I could catch up financially.

SO BY 2001, I was looking eye to eye with success. "Who'd have believed it?" we liked to say. Reasonable success is hard to describe, especially when you didn't actually set out to obtain it. After all, who would go to Idaho to achieve their financial dreams? Lots of people hardly know where Idaho is.

I saw the lives of my wife, our children and myself somewhat like a train that took a long time to get rolling but had gained a lot of momentum. Regular maintenance and tending was important, and I had learned the nuances of its personality. Hopefully, with proper and responsible care, this train would arrive safely at the retirement station with a decent load of cargo, our children with a good start in life, and our having completed a somewhat long and arduous journey.

There is much more to this story, meaning that I was not so responsible for our success that I should receive much credit. I'll talk about that elsewhere and add other details, because it is important. The point here is that we could essentially write a check for whatever we really wanted, which was not anything we could not write a check for. One equals one, and we were there, financially independent, owing no one a dime. Many people arrive somewhere and don't realize it. From my perspective, we had arrived and I knew it. I thanked God for my blessings, my daughters, my business, our house, our toys, good health and so much more.

Why then, what happened, what possessed me to cry out to Him while I was driving around Crays' corner that late winter in 2001? What was dying inside me that was gasping for a breath of life? What had God started so long ago that was lying neglected inside this man who had become a religious facsimile of one originally enamored with such an amazing God? What finally caused all the words He had spoken concerning a significant purpose for my life to rise up and appear before me like some ghost from a forgotten past?

I don't know, but as I drove to work that day I suddenly cried, "Ah! Lord!!! Where are you? Where did you go? Something is dreadfully wrong here!! I have all of this stuff, but where are you? Please, hear me! Help me!"

THEN I SAID it. I'm sure it was one prayer He heard. It must have been that. It must have started with this prayer, this simple prayer, "Lord, I don't want to sacrifice an ounce of eternity for a ton of the present. I mean it. Help me!"

Bingo. Within less than two years I lost, chronologically, our motorcycling friends, my wife, my ability to sleep without drugs, our home, my business, a job, several trusted friends, and contact with my children. I ended up alone in Denver with nothing to do. I had heard the worst things said to me by friends, business associates and others. I had been insulted and felt betrayed by those I trusted the most. And though God hung around at first, He too seemed to have had enough of me and disappeared. I know the Bible says that He will never leave or forsake us, but from my perspective, He seemed strangely absent. People told me to cheer up, that things couldn't get much worse. They did.

I was going to learn to walk with Him in a new way, but there are some details to fill in.

4

The Crash

I love to dream and I dream often. I have occasionally even been aware in my dreams that I'm only dreaming and jumped off high places, walked through fire, or flown into the sky. Nightmares are a different experience.

THURSDAY, JANUARY 3, 2002, I arrive home from a regular day at work. As usual, I'm glad to be home. Though my wife's vehicle is not there, I figure she'll be back soon. I liked seeing her when I came home from work and she usually tried to be there. But now, there is something different as I climb the stairs from the basement after parking in the garage. Things are missing. Something's not right. I feel it, but I shrug it off.

That feeling is like seeing the doctor for a checkup. You're fine. The doctor examines you and leaves for a few minutes. When he returns, he looks upset. There is concern in his forced smile, but you suppose it's not about you. Perhaps he heard something about someone else that disturbed him. Or maybe you're on your way home from shopping and you notice smoke in the distance. It occurs to you that your house is in that area, but you dismiss it.

I find a note on the table near our kitchen, a piece of paper torn from a yellow legal pad. *I've left for a while. Call in a couple of weeks* is hastily scribbled on it. What? What could this be about? Our children? Her sister? Then I look around and find lots of things missing, all of her personal belongings. What is going on?

Or perhaps the doctor says that you have a lump he needs to look at, do a biopsy. What could this be about? As you drive closer, the smoke is definitely billowing up from where your house could be. What?! Could it be possible?

I go down to the barn. The horses ... gone. The trailer ... gone. Back to the house. The office files ... gone. Computer ... gone. We had chickens. They're ... *gone*. I'm reeling, stunned.

The doctor does the biopsy. He says, "You have cancer." Cancer? You turn the corner and there's your house—on fire. No fire trucks. Nothing. It's just burning by itself. Has anyone called? Does anyone care that your house is on fire? The neighbors, where are they?

None of this seems possible for me. I don't get cancer, my house doesn't burn down and my wife of twenty-six years doesn't take all of her personal belongings and leave for two weeks without mentioning it. Not a word. No warning.

We'll get through this, I think. She's just upset. We'll talk it out. Why would she do this? Is this my fault? Can't be cancer. None in my family. There's no reason for cancer. Why would my house be on fire? We had everything inspected. I left no burners on. Somebody else must have done something. Why would someone set my house on fire? Did she warn me? I can't remember. Should I call our children? Should I involve them? I don't know.

I need to let some time pass, let the emotional surge subside, if it will, so that I can possibly think somewhat clearly. I pass the weekend by driving all the way to another state to visit a friend in Sheridan, Wyoming.

The following Monday morning, I stand at my front window and watch as Cathie's best friend drives up our long driveway. She gets out of her car and approaches our front door cautiously, obviously not sure of my frame of mind. I let her in and invite her to sit down. We sit across from each other at the table. She stares at me, trying to read me. I know this is going to be bad, and I believe that this friend assisted my wife's flight. I feel like the victim of a conspiracy.

"What's going on?" I ask, glaring at her.

"Cathie has left you. You can't fix this. I wouldn't even try," she says quickly, bravely, and she waits for my reaction. I'm big. She's just a small woman, so I'm impressed with her courage. I like courage, which she is displaying. She took the chance, the initiative, had the decency to face me and give me some clue about what was happening. I probably never liked her too much before, but right now I see something to admire. I decide to listen.

"Okay, and you probably won't tell me where she is."
"No," she says firmly.

Somehow I realize that I am defeated, done. There is no fight in me. I don't argue with her. The cancer and the fire are real. They aren't going to simply go away. I'm fairly used to crises. I don't like them, but I assume that somehow I'll handle this one too—or so I imagined.

"Any suggestions?" I ask.
"Let her think. Don't pressure her."
"Okay … and thanks."

I try to follow her suggestion. My performance is mixed. Cathie *is* still my wife, and this is new territory. One friend insists that I go get her. It worked for him. Another cautions me to leave her alone. Yet another assures me that she will return, if I decide to become a better person—as if I had been choosing to be a bad one. Emotions peak all around, and the Enemy comes in a flood.

I HAVE EXPERIENCED occasional nightmares. Normally I lie down to sleep, expecting to wake in the morning. Suddenly I am having a nightmare. Why is what I'm experiencing so frightening? I should know that what I'm seeing and feeling is not normal, but I accept it. What's wrong with me that I let nightmares terrify me? Such visions aren't normal, yet my brain continues to process the information. I see things that can't be, and I experience fear and anxiety over seemingly impossible visions. Nightmares should be recognized as irrational, but I'm still afraid. Fortunately, I eventually awake, and the nightmare is gone and quickly forgotten.

Now, in this new reality, it is the opposite. Now, everything is reversed. Life is better when I'm asleep. Somehow, with the help of drugs,

I manage to sleep. But I awake to the nightmare. I awake in the middle of the night expecting my wife to be in bed next to me, where she has always been for nearly half of my life. But now she's not. Why not? Is she away? We were hardly ever away from each other. We didn't take separate vacations. Other than for a few of my business trips, we went everywhere together. Why isn't she here? Oh, I forgot. We're in the middle of a divorce. She has left me. I forgot, again. The nightmare materializes as I awaken. I have traded places with a nightmare. Sleep is now much better. It doesn't hurt when I'm asleep. The waking up is what hurts, trying to put my new reality, my nightmare, together.

Acceptance does not come easily. It has to be forced. I can acknowledge reality with my brain, but it takes a lot of time for my new situation to become real enough to stay with me, to not require extra effort to recognize as true, to become normal. But I don't want this to become normal. I don't like this kind of normal. Normal is married with my children safe and some money in the bank. I've worked for that normalcy. Why would someone, especially someone I have been with for so long, want to change this?

We don't give people cancer and we don't set people's houses on fire. What was wrong with our marriage? Was there a problem? It wasn't perfect, but whose is? What exactly did I do to cause her to leave without a single warning? Is there something I can do to stop our relationship from disintegrating? Do I accept this? If I accept something, does that mean I quit trying to make it different? If I'm diagnosed with cancer, what does acceptance mean? Certainly, I want to try to get well. I don't concede defeat for a minute. If my house is slowly burning, do I run inside and try to salvage something? Where are the firemen? What do I do here? Do I just stand by and watch my house burn down?

People tell me that I have to accept that she's gone. How do I accept that? Do I quit trying or hoping to get her back? Is that what it means to accept? I don't know what to do or how to handle anything. I didn't plan on this. Who would? Who would plan on divorce? We're Christians. Christians are supposed to work things out. We didn't do a prenuptial agreement. That's how people plan for divorce, I guess. I trusted her with everything. Now she took our money and got an attorney to sue me! How did I become so untrustworthy as to require suing? Have I done something dishonest to my family? Now *I* need an attorney to defend myself! No, this is not a good thing to accept.

I don't appreciate some comments from Christian friends: "You've been a bully. You never loved her. You can't remarry, you know. That would be adultery. You'll have to live alone for the rest of your life. God will bring her back, if that's His will."

Normal people don't say you deserved to have your house burn. Friends don't say that you deserved cancer. Nobody says things like that. But from my perspective, some people seem to imply I deserved this.

DIVORCE IS COMMON now. I cannot imagine the life of a divorcee fifty years ago. I can't imagine the lives of slaves, or the lives of people who suffer under brutal dictators. I can't comprehend the fear and pain of Christians persecuted in intolerant countries. I can't possibly have a valid concept of the absolutely horrible things that people have endured since this planet first held life. Who even *wants* to think about those things? We may stare momentarily at someone who is disfigured, or at an automobile wreck. But we can't feel like those people. We don't want to feel like those people. Who would? We like to feel good. We're made to feel pleasure. People say to me that they *know how I feel.* How can they? How can *anybody* know how someone else feels? I can't know how others feel. I can't even imagine my own pain unless I actually feel it.

I enjoy adrenaline activities like pushing myself on a pedal bike ride. I can look at a hill and imagine how I'm going to just pedal right on up that thing. Yet halfway up the hill, when the nausea and gasping are really peaking, I often wonder why I do such things. It seemed okay at the bottom. Before I start up the hill, my brain knows that I will not be feeling well halfway up the hill, but there is no reality to it. Otherwise, I might avoid the hill. The pain is not realized until it is actually felt. But that kind of pain is acceptable because it is related to an activity, a purpose, and is momentary.

The pain of divorce seems purposeless, pointless. The anxiety and the difficult breathing come out of nowhere. There is no hill I'm attempting to climb. I can't see anything to relate the pain to, no purpose to attach it to.

A couple of times during the worst attacks, I think about checking myself into the hospital, but I go instead to an old friend, Art. We sit together for hours. "Breathe, Jonathan," he says, staring at me. The anxiety becomes manageable for a while. My breathing returns to normal. He has never seen me this way. Neither have I. I've handled so many crises, but I don't know this fearful person I have now become.

I had never, ever in my life, with all that we had been through together, ever expected to be left by Cathie.

ONE SATURDAY A few weeks later, as I sat alone in my house, I saw a vision of the outline of a roof. Some type of building was being presented to me, and I knew it was in Lewiston, seventy miles north. The next day, Sunday, I dressed for church and drove to where I could get a clear view of Lewiston's skyline. There was a building on a hill with the same roof line. I drove there and discovered a church, which I attended for the next six months as I waited for the divorce to become final. The Lord had His purpose for that too. I had no idea that an old friend was attending the church. We had lost track of each other. The Lord, I guess, knew it would be better to send me to another town for some comfort and a change of venue.

THEY SAY THAT divorce is worse than death, because there is no finality in divorce. The anger, criticism, accusations and rejection often continue for years, leaving deep wounds that may never heal. The "dumper," the one initiating the divorce, who essentially gets what they think they wanted, usually fares better than the "dumpee," the one being divorced. The dumpers find enough for which to blame on the other to justify their actions and go on with life. The dumpee doesn't do so well. Both supposedly get what they deserved.

Everybody liked Cathie. I was not so well liked. I was intimidating and arrogant, according to some. She was pretty and caring, a wonderful wife, and she gave me two wonderful children. I worked hard and played hard. She did lots of things for others. She helped me with everything and always stood beside me when my sometimes dumb ideas and plans failed to work. I thought we were a team, as I dragged her back and forth across the country, spent money I shouldn't have and probably paid more attention to what was important to me than to her.

I supposed it was true. I got what I deserved. She deserved better. I tried to get that into my mind. Now I had to move on, try to figure things out and hope for another chance. Period.

As people, we are usually trying to get what we deserve. Our prisons contain many people who think they *don't* deserve to be there. So I've heard. Maybe they actually got what they deserved. I don't know. Most of us might think we deserve to be paid more. When I had employees, I'm sure many felt that way. Some of them said so. Most of us like to buy low and sell high. We somehow feel that we deserve a better deal than we are offered. Though my employees wanted to be paid more, they usually wanted to pay less for groceries. Many people living in Grangeville drive seventy miles north to a larger town, rather than pay the generally higher prices charged locally. They like to live locally though. If a local store goes out of business, well, they got what they deserved.

I didn't like having to determine the standard of living for my employees. I was never sure how to determine what they deserved to be paid, so I used the prevailing wage rate as a guide. It seemed arbitrary, but who was I to argue with capitalism? I appreciate people who work and produce actual things. I never minded physically working, which managing was not, to me. You think that when you work hard, people will appreciate your effort. You think that you deserve reasonable compensation for your labor.

Statistically, I knew my chances of avoiding divorce were roughly even. But I tried to follow the rules, so I thought I deserved to be stayed with, to be lived with for the rest of my life. I tried to believe the right things, do the right things and say the right things. I don't know. I didn't fool around, hang out with the guys, or abuse my wife. I *thought* I did the right things.

I'm sure Cathie would tell a different story. I've watched too many wives roll their eyes while confident husbands described the bliss of their marriage. In the divorce recovery meetings I went to and elsewhere, I heard tales of horrible marriages. The problems I experienced in my marriage seemed tame in comparison. So I didn't see a valid reason for being divorced, for being treated as a piece of unwanted trash and for being sued like a violator of someone's rights.

I also began to realize that most of my thoughts and reflections were about *me*, such as, *how could she do this to me?* It was not right, I concluded, to be thinking that way. I was not proud of a lot of my thoughts. Maybe she was right. Maybe it *was* always all about me. How could I be so selfish, so clueless? Maybe we *both* got what we deserved. I had no idea anymore.

SOMEWHERE ALONG THE line a magazine article caught my attention. The symptoms of depression were listed on the front cover. After reading the list, I decided that I was depressed and went to my doctor, thinking that I would have to convince him to let me have some drugs. What I really needed was help sleeping. Sleep, my refuge from the pain, had fled along with my family. I pictured batteries of tests, referrals to a psychologist or psychiatrist, and hours of unpleasant probing and questioning.

"Here. Try this," he said after a brief discussion, and he handed me free samples of one of the popular new antidepressants. It didn't work.

Ultimately, though I went through three doctors and probably ten different drugs or drug combinations for nearly eight months, nothing helped me feel better. The side effects, nervousness, jitters, and more anxiety were all I got. I was taking three times the recommended adult dose of a powerful sleep aid to get barely six blessed hours of sleep a night. So much for science.

THE LORD BEGAN to speak to me again during that difficult spring of 2002 . I was not aware that He had been strangely silent for a long time, actually for years. Suddenly, He indicated to me that a particular Bible passage was an explanation, of sorts, regarding my situation. It was an unfamiliar passage, but as I read it, the implications were ominous.

> "Of whom were you worried and fearful,
> When you lied, and did not remember Me,
> Nor give Me a thought?
> Was I not silent even for a long time
> So you do not fear Me?
> I will declare your righteousness and your deeds,
> But they will not profit you.
> When you cry out, let your collection of idols deliver you.
> But the wind will carry all of them up,
> And a breath will take them away.

But he who takes refuge in Me shall inherit the land,
And shall possess My holy mountain."

And it shall be said,
"Build up, build up, prepare the way,
Remove every obstacle out of the way of My people."

For thus says the high and exalted One
Who lives forever, whose name is Holy,
"I dwell on a high and holy place,
And also with the contrite and lowly of spirit
In order to revive the spirit of the lowly
And to revive the heart of the contrite.
For I will not contend forever,
Neither will I always be angry;
For the spirit would grow faint before Me,
And the breath of those whom I have made.
Because of the iniquity of his unjust gain I was angry and struck him;
I hid My face and was angry,
And he went on turning away, in the way of his heart.
I have seen his ways, but I will heal him.
I will lead him and restore comfort to him and to his mourners,
Creating the praise of the lips." (Isaiah 57:11–19)

Though there is more in the above scripture regarding my situation than is appropriate to discuss, it was at least partly relevant. I had quite a collection of toys. Were they idols? Was it the money? But had my gain been unjust? What did He mean by that? Was that really for me? He had not spoken to me for a long time. Had I angered Him? Had He struck me? Was this nightmare orchestrated by God to serve His purpose in some way?

ONE EVENING AS I sat alone, I had a vision of a large boat floating fairly high on calm waters. There was an obvious hole in its side above the waterline.

"You are like this boat," the Lord implied. *"As long as the seas are*

calm and the load is light, you are okay. I want to take you through some rough waters and have you carry a heavy load. The hole needs to be fixed."

I figured that a simple patch job would do, but God doesn't do patches. I knew that. He is not about fixing up the old. There is a popular song called "The Potter's Hand." It seems nice to sing songs about God's intervening in our lives, breaking and remaking us in His image, and there is a lot of good preaching and teaching available on the process. That spring, I listened to a loud preacher almost daring God to come into his life and bring down His heavenly bulldozer to clear away every impediment to His perfect will. I remember it well. He clearly boasted about it. While some of the congregation gave their hearty agreement, I quietly slid lower in my seat. No, God doesn't do patches. First He tears down. Way down. That heavenly bulldozer can come out of nowhere to rip up, tear down and destroy everything dear to a person.

Prior to the widespread use of chemicals, it was common for land to be fallowed for a season or perhaps several. That way, every last seed would be sure to germinate. The ground could be plowed under several times until there were no remaining seeds. As I drove to church one evening, He offered another relevant word, *"I will finish this."* It was clear. This was a hands-off job. God was taking over and I could do nothing but hang on. I had no idea how rough the ride would get. I was not aware that the Lord would plow my soil for not one, but for *many* seasons—for *years.*

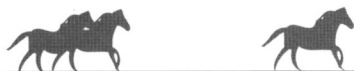

AS IS COMMON in business partnerships, there had been some friction between my partner and me in our twelve years, but I was not prepared for the next falling shoe. I was the first to suggest a split, for unrelated reasons, not long after my wife left. Later, I reconsidered, and by that summer of 2002, I was looking forward to some stability and meaningful hard work. Now, *he* wanted a split. Didn't anybody want me around? We struggled some, but after a friend offered me an opportunity in Wyoming, it seemed better that I sell my half and move on. Wyoming seemed like it might be a good place to go to lick my wounds. I had already left the house we had prayed about, built and managed to pay for, which had been my home for ten years. I was living in a studio apartment. It was not difficult to throw what I had left in another U-Haul and move to Sheridan, Wyoming.

Though Grangeville was remote, I enjoyed our small-town existence. So I looked forward to making a life in Sheridan, also small and remote. There are fine people there who enjoy their town, but, I guess for me, it just wasn't meant to be.

It began with the train, or rather the house. The men I was joining on a business project provided me with a furnished house, which was a nice idea since I had no furniture.

SHERIDAN IS SITUATED partly on the side of a hill that opens to the vastness of eastern Wyoming. Trains carry coal and other products along tracks that run north and south along the east side of the town. As I first drove into Sheridan early that fall, I spotted the tracks, and a small wheel in my mind turned sufficiently to flip a small switch, which lighted a dim, red bulb. The little light barely caught my attention and was quickly forgotten. I proceeded toward the office address and was soon escorted to the house, a dark, forties-vintage, brick five-bedroom. It looked like an institutional building where old people who chased children away by swatting at them with their canes would live.

"How do you like it? Pretty nice, huh? Think it will work?" my friend asked as he showed me around the fortress.

"Nice," I lied. "It will do just fine. Thanks."

"Get moved in and call me in a couple. We'll start going over things."

"Sounds good. I'll call you day after tomorrow."

The house was monstrous. Where in this cavernous dwelling would I make my lonely little existence? Certainly not in one of the huge upstairs bedrooms with overstuffed chairs and king-size beds. Besides, did they get this furniture out of a castle in Transylvania? Thick, heavy, dark-oak headboards, dressers and night stands adorned with ugly, black, wrought-iron hinges and spiked things filled the huge, small-windowed rooms. The decor could only be described as early Inquisition style. Instead, I found a small room on the main floor and moved in a single bed with a few reasonable pieces from other parts of the house. Then I went to sleep—for a couple of hours.

It was sometime around midnight, I guess. *WOOOOOOOOO! WOOO-OOOO!! WOOO! WOO!!!*

What was that?! The train! I was a light sleeper. Trains are dangerous for light sleepers. That little red, light was suddenly shining brightly now as I remembered the motel we had stopped at years ago. Yes, it was Sheridan. It was late. We had gotten a room. Sometime shortly after we fell asleep, the trains had started. It was incredible. The tracks ran directly behind the motel. Who would put a motel there? Could anyone sleep in such a place?

Twice again that night a train ran through Sheridan. I slept little. The next day I discovered that the house was strategically situated so as to have a nearly clear view overlooking the tracks, perhaps three hundred yards away. Between were just the scant limbs of a few hardwoods. If trains aren't already noisy enough, their air horns are an engineering marvel actually capable of overcoming five hundred-plus watts of rap music blaring from the cabin of a well-insulated, custom low-rider. "Hey!!" the horns scream. "Several hundred tons of steel and stuff on wheels comin' at you, baby!!" There were apparently five crossings in Sheridan, and the trains ran about three times a night with probably five horn blasts per crossing. I did the math. Seventy-five blasts per night was a problem that needed an immediate solution.

First, at a local drugstore, I purchased a couple pairs of the highest db-rated earplugs I could find, thinking an extra pair might be handy. Would two plugs fit one ear? Maybe, but probably not. Unfortunately, the earplugs, though they helped, were insufficient, and the following night was nearly as sleepless. Second, I discovered that the house had a very large walk-in closet centered upstairs. I moved a couple of mattresses in. The next evening I went into the closet, closed the door and went to sleep. The trains were now a memory. This would work. It was suffocating, but it was quiet.

"How are you liking the house?" my business associates asked.

"Great," I lied again.

"Good. So, let's get down to business."

"Say," I asked casually, opening my notebook, "do the trains ever bother you guys?"

"Trains? No. Why? Why would the trains bother us?" they replied, exchanging frowns and giving me peculiar looks.

"Nothing. Never mind," I answered quickly.

"Good. Now here's the way I think we should proceed …"

The only other problem to be solved regarding the house was the Humvee, the military version of the Hummer, sitting in the garage. The house had twin basement garages separated by a brick structural wall with a small man-door. Other than the segmented bay doors, there was no garage access except through the basement. I needed garage access for my motorcycles and shop work. I like tools. I work on stuff. But the Humvee was parked in the garage next to the basement. To get to my work area, I would have to go from the basement into the first garage, skinny around the vehicle, which nearly filled the available space, and enter the empty garage. No good.

Though the owner said the Humvee could be moved, I would have to do it myself. No problem, I thought. Start it up and drive it out. Maybe.

I played with the totally unfamiliar switches and buttons. It wouldn't turn over. Dead battery, no doubt. I know nothing about Humvees, but apparently this was either one of the first ones to roll off the assembly line or a prototype of some sort. It appeared absolutely ancient, had been well used and three tires were nearly flat. While trying to locate the battery, I discovered the absence of plug wires, which was disheartening. It was a diesel. I know diesels. Diesels can be very tricky to get running, especially when they're worn out, and this thing was well past seed stage. Maybe I would leave it and just work around it. No, maybe I'd move it.

Eventually I located the batteries, attached a charger, and headed to the parts store for starter fluid. Chances were perfect that it wouldn't fire without help. I returned, and with both the charger and my car battery attached, sprayed starter fluid in the air intake and engaged the starter. It spun pretty well and eventually lit on a couple of cylinders, but it would not keep running. The smoke was incredible.

The amount of dense, gray smoke a worn-out diesel can generate is amazing. The gray cloud billowed from the stubbed exhaust pipe underneath and filled the area outside the garages. I waited for the inside area to clear and re-entered. After a few tries and additional starter fluid, the old motor was firing on enough cylinders to run by itself, but it was still producing gobs of smoke. I dashed back in the garage hoping to get the vehicle to move before someone called the fire department. It took several choking and gasping attempts before I could figure out how to get it into reverse. Finally, the transmission engaged and the Humvee crawled backwards. I prayed that the fire trucks were not on their way. I might need lung surgery down the road, but I had my garage.

THE DEAL IN Sheridan did not work. *Why* is not important. They had their opinions and I had mine. No need to explain. In business, different people have different ways of accomplishing things. Their way was not my way, and in a couple of months I headed for Denver. Now unemployed, my situation had deteriorated further. Maybe things would go better in Denver.

I stayed in contact with some of my former friends, though many avoided me as if divorce were a contagious disease. I thanked the Lord for my cell phone. With all of the moving, the phone became my lifeline. I often spent hours on it, mostly just to pass time.

I'm not a cynic. I wouldn't have experienced the successes I have had in life as a cynic. But I'm no dreamer either. I've had plenty of experience with plans not working out. Sometimes a better plan emerges, sometimes life becomes difficult. I had experienced trauma once in the form of complete financial loss, which I'll go into later. I know that situations can improve, but they can also go from bad to worse. Though nearly everybody tried to be encouraging, I came to appreciate understanding more than so-called encouragement. I received welcome understanding from a few whose lives had been irrevocably altered by trauma. But it was as if I were wrong in doubting the rosy scenario that, according to others, was just around the next corner.

5

Denver

How fast you go or how high you fly doesn't matter. When you crash, the sudden stop is what hurts. Then there is the resulting hole.

B RAD, IN HIS many forms, was usually around somewhere, either at a church, or as both old and new acquaintances.

"Things are going to get better real soon, Jonathan. You can bank on it."

"Really, Brad? You think so?"

"Yep. I have a feeling about these things. I know. It's in the bag."

"You're sure?"

"Sure, I'm sure. Listen. I know that nothing has gone right for you for a while, but this is different. God is going to bless your socks off, and it is right around the corner."

"Is it a tight corner or a wide, sweeping one, or maybe a U-turn or something? Maybe a circle? I mean, I've heard this before."

"What?"

"That things were going to get better. Seems like they keep getting worse."

"Come on, buddy. You've just got to believe. Have some faith. Drop all this negative garbage and you'll see what I'm talking about. Okay?"

"Well, sort of okay. Hey, so you're real sure about this? I mean like a real, sure thing?"

"You bet. Double bank on it. Real soon, bro, real soon."

"Double bank on it?"

"Double, maybe triple."

"Really."

"I'm believing for it, man. Trust me."

"Sure?"

"Absolutely."

"Like maybe a thousand dollars sure?"

"Uh, what? What are you talking about? What's a thousand dollars?"

"Well, I just thought you might want to put some money behind your sureness."

"Money?"

"Yeah, money, dollars, hard currency. Yeah, I like this. See, if things get better, I would gladly pay you a thousand dollars. But if they don't, your thousand would help make me feel a little better. I mean, there are five things that I would like some movement on, and if I could get somewhere on only two, the thousand to you would be nothing. If you're so sure, why not put some money behind it?"

"Are you kidding?"

"No. I'm liking the idea the more I think about it. I'm even *feeling* better just thinking about it. Yeah. It's like you and others think that if I could simply see things your better way, all this bad stuff would just disappear. Put some money behind your so-called encouragement."

"You're weird, you know. Here I am just trying to help you, and you get weird. No wonder. You shouldn't look at things that way. Money."

"Why?"

"Because it isn't right. You know? I'm feeling something that might be from the Lord, and you put a price on it. You shouldn't do that. Some people would get offended, but I love you, so I'm not getting offended here. Okay?"

"Yeah, okay."

"You hang in there. You'll see. Hey, I gotta go. You take care now, and let me know. Don't be a stranger. Call me, okay?"

"Okay. See ya."

"Take care, man."

As he left, I mumbled, "Two thousand would be even more encouragement."

"You say something?" he remarked, looking over his shoulder. "Nope, nothin', see ya."

WHY DID I decide to move to Denver? It was close? I had an old friend there? I'm not sure, but I planned on making something come together, either a job or a business. The truth is, I had no idea where else to go. Sheridan was not a good place to be sitting around single. My parents had passed away; and though a brother and two sisters lived near Baltimore, I wasn't ready to return to the East Coast. Normally I would find work first, but I wanted someplace to come home to.

I loaded my stuff into another U-Haul, drove to Denver, rented a townhouse and asked Gary's wife to help me pick out some furniture. Gary, who lived just outside Denver, had led me to the Lord near Grangeville in 1977.

"What type of furniture are you looking for?" she asked.

"I don't know." Strange. My father had owned a large furniture store and I had worked there for several summers as a kid. But I still know nothing about furniture, one of the many environmental aspects that seemed to escape my notice so often.

For example, back in Grangeville around 1991, we owned a home in a small subdivision. I was annoyed and kept awake at night by a next-door neighbor's barking dog. Though we tried to work something out with them, they weren't interested. There were *two* windows in our bedroom and one faced the neighbors directly. Now, keep in mind that my wife Cathie and I had done a lot of remodeling together. After dinner one evening she was standing in the bedroom as I entered.

"Notice anything different?" she inquired.

I was alarmed. A test. I eyed her up and down. Nothing stood out, though I was sure that something was supposed to. What could it be? I felt tense. Hair? Nothing there. I mean, nothing different. Makeup? Clothes?

"Not me. The bedroom! ... Notice anything different?" she continued. Her mouth widened into a smile, though her eyes just watched me. I think Cathie always hoped I would be better than I was. They say that men marry women hoping they will never change, and women marry men hoping they will. I remained unchanged apparently, visually unobservant. If men are supposed to be so visual, I was failing the gender, at least concerning my surroundings.

"The bedroom, Jonathan. Something's changed."

Relieved, I had another chance. I looked around. Furniture? That was pretty simple. Check. Wall paint? Check, though I could be wrong. Drapes? Did we have drapes? I can't remember. Bedspread? Pillows? Carpet? Who knows? I could not see a thing that had changed. "I don't see anything," I said, feeling warm.

"You're kidding," she said, shaking her head with amusement.

"Give me a hint." I was roadkill.

"The window."

"Okay …" I looked at the window. I saw a window, *one* window. Nothing new there.

"There were *two* of them!" she exclaimed.

"Yes, yes. Of course. *Two* windows!" I conceded, but I couldn't really remember. Hey, we'd only been there a year. Give me a break. It takes time to figure *everything* out. "There's only one," I said sheepishly.

"I removed the window today. I thought it would help you sleep," she said proudly, gesturing with her arm toward the now windowless wall.

Can you believe this? I am not lying. Between the time I left for work and the time I got home, she had moved the furniture, removed the window, studded the opening, sheeted the outside, insulated, attached a piece of sheetrock, taped, textured, painted the surface, and replaced the furniture. What a wife! She did things like that for me. Am I clueless or what? I guess I did get what I deserved.

"How do you want it to look?"

"What?"

"Earth calling Jonathan. Your Denver townhouse. We're picking out furniture. How do you want it to look?"

"Nice."

"What?"

"I want it to look nice. Like Cathie would make it look. She always made everything look nice. She could take so little and make so much out of it. She made our home look really nice, always."

"You miss her."

"You know? I really just want to go home, but I don't know where home is. I used to know, but now I don't. That's all."

"Maybe it would be good for you to pick out the furniture yourself. Maybe you'll be inspired to do your thing."

"Bad idea. My thing is machines. I don't want my place to resemble a machine. I want it to look homey, like somebody who knew what they were doing picked out the furniture. Your home is nice. Make it look like yours, except …"

"Except what?"

"Not too many flowers. You know …"

"Got it. Not too many flowers. You're going to be okay. Come on. Let's go take a look. There's a huge store here."

So I bought some furniture.

IN DENVER, I was looking eye to eye with … what? I didn't know. I had no clue as to what the future might be, where I was headed or what might happen next. I had been a husband, father, business owner, provider, companion, counselor, worship leader, Bible teacher, and landowner. Now who was I? None of those. I spent the winter looking for jobs and businesses without success. It was a long winter, my first alone ever in my life, but the Lord spoke to me a few times.

One Monday toward the end of the winter, just over a year after the nightmare began, I was sitting in my townhouse when the Lord said to me directly, *"I will make a way for you."*

A way for me? A way where? Was another move coming? The next day, Gary stopped by on his way home from work. God spoke to Gary.

"He said to tell you that it's an enigma," Gary said. Gary did not use words like *enigma*.

"Huh? What?"

"I was driving along today and the Lord said, 'Tell Jonathan it's an enigma.' Why would He say that?"

"Well, here's why," I replied. "Last Sunday I was in Utah, driving along Interstate 70, talking to a woman about life. I used the term *enigma* three times in part of our conversation. I remember it clearly. So God's letting me know He was there, listening. No doubt, brother, He speaks to you."

"Well, here's something else. I believe He also told me that your winding, obstacle-filled road is about to become straight."

"Interesting."

AND IT WAS for a while. In a few weeks a light appeared on the horizon, and it would be one of the lights that I would chase during the next few years hoping to find a warm fire and friends, and a place to settle and rebuild my life. Some of the lights were fires which burned for some time, though they all seemed to eventually go out. Sheridan never really got started. Denver burned only briefly. This one would burn for a few years, though it would need some fuel.

While rummaging around on the Internet for a business to buy, I contacted a former friend who had sold manufacturing equipment to us during my twelve-year partnership. I was looking for information on local machine purchases. The contact resulted in my moving to Coeur d'Alene, Idaho, investing in his business and buying a house.

I lived and did something comparable to work in Coeur d'Alene for three and a half years. I met a lot of people, went to several churches, traveled a lot and had a lot of conversations with people and some with God. Though I was lonely and life seemed pointless, God was teaching me many things, some things I was hesitant to learn.

He began showing up in unusual ways and saying unusual things.

6

Living Among Ashes

Did you know that ashes can be used to make soap, which helps us get clean; fertilizer, which helps things grow; and as one of the ingredients in cinder building blocks? Anyone who has had the opportunity to visit the area around Mt. St. Helens, Washington knows the awesome power of nature. The scope of the devastation is difficult to convey with mere words or pictures. Yet even after such near annihilation, life has risen among the ashes. It sure looks different though. Sure does.

THE WORDS CAME out of thin air in the early spring of 2004 as I was approaching an intersection in Coeur d'Alene, *"See? Just because your life sucks doesn't mean that you can't make someone else's life better."*

"Are You supposed to be using words like that?" was my immediate nonverbal response. God was using language that I deemed not fitting for Him to use. *Sucks* was not a word that I believed fit into a vocabulary remotely associated with any divine being, much less our Holy Father, who gave His son for us.

Yet the implication was there, *"Are you going to use your standards to judge what is acceptable for Me to say?"* It was Him, His voice, His presence, His personality, but, to me, just not His vocabulary.

I still shudder a bit even writing about this. It seems so out of place. Sometimes, when I've mentioned incidents like this to others, it's not hard to infer from the looks I get, "Sure, Jonathan. Sure. Whatever."

I had just dropped off a never-used two-year-old dirt bike at a coworker's. We had decided to give some bonuses in the form of motorcycles to promote togetherness among our business team. It made owning a *technically* new toy easier for a good guy. He was absolutely literally jumped up in the air with glee. I had gone to some fairly serious trouble to find just the right bike, worked a super deal that probably left me owing a bit to an old friend, and had driven several hundred miles to pick up and deliver the thing.

My life was still not acceptable to me, at least, and I was not always delighted to see others quite so happy. According to His own words, even God agreed that my life, well, sucked. (That's actually hard to write down.) So I was not so good around happy people whose lives were going well. "Go be happy somewhere else, please," I would think, half out loud. But it was true, I could still contribute, function, be a positive asset to someone else's life, if I wanted to—I guess I wanted to.

THERE IS AN understanding among guys who tend to compete with each other. It goes like this. I really want you to do well. I really do. I just don't want you to do too well, like better than me. Okay? I want you to find a better job, but not better than mine. I like you to ride fast on your bike; fast, that is, behind me. Are we clear here? Buddy?

I understand that a competitive attitude isn't acceptable or fitting for a Christian. It still exists too often. You can be too successful for your friends and even your church. Many of us, especially guys, like to surround ourselves with others who reinforce our beliefs and values, who make us feel comfortable with who we are and what we are doing. Few of us like to hear critical words concerning our abilities, mannerisms, accomplishments, family, or anything of personal significance. Direct attacks are not welcome. But we can also feel personally attacked by being confronted by someone who is better at something we value, by someone who is experiencing success. So after my divorce, I was not pleased to be around people who were happy, doing better than I was. Competition is rampant among us adult male Christians. It's wrong, and jealousy is a big part of it. It's a sin, and we should repent.

Jesus made the Pharisees look bad, though that's only part of the story. He actually did what they merely talked about. When others expose our deficiencies or failures, we have options. We can acknowledge their strengths and successes or we can employ countermeasures. We can call attention to our superiority in areas we regard as more significant in an attempt to reduce the other person to our level, or we can counterattack by drawing attention to their deficiencies, hopefully damaging their credibility.

These countermeasures are sometimes called survival techniques, which are the strategies we employ as a means for self-preservation or ways of justifying our positions. Also, by controlling our environment, we can sometimes manage to completely avoid criticism and exposure. Many tend to stratify aspects of their lives into discreet layers, thereby providing some "insulation" from intrusions from above and below. For example, we might justify our particular economic position by implying that people on a lower economic level don't work as hard or are not as good at stewardship. Therefore, we feel that our better lifestyle is deserved.

As Christians, we should rejoice when others succeed, do better, or even surpass us. Though competition is acceptable and appropriate in recreation, when it carries over into our personal and social relationships, competition should be a warning that there is a fundamental problem of jealousy abiding in us, even though our exterior life appears so acceptable. Perhaps we are even guilty of idolatry in some ways.

We can even extend this self-preservation strategy to insulate ourselves from intrusion by God Himself. We can listen to what pleases us, reinforces us and comforts us. We might regard those who appear to be more obedient to the Lord as probably not realizing the pressures we are under. We might convince ourselves that some compromises are necessary, and certainly God understands. We are assured by our church leaders that God will always forgive, though we are still admonished to try to keep some standard which varies from church to church.

This mysterious standard of righteousness exists too often in modern churches that preach grace and love. Everyone seems to acknowledge that no one really keeps the mysterious standard, but only a few are willing to confess *specifically how* they fail to keep the standard, which I will address later.

We can also claim to see clearly, to understand everything and to be a leader of sightless others and, according to Jesus, be considered blind, or we can admit our blindness, realize that there is so much we fail to see and trust God to lead us. It can be very scary—losing control, that is. But losing control means trusting God, placing everything in His hands, under His control.

Not that many of us mortals really get a bona fide opportunity to put everything, every part of our lives into God's hands. Who would want to? Control is important to us. Besides, there's that troublesome *cross* issue and those annoying statements Jesus made about self-denial.

I often thought about how fortunate I was in one way. No family, no dependents, no real commitments. I was truly alone. I was contributing little to our business in Coeur d'Alene. I knew that. Perhaps, now, for once, I could let God have complete control.

Let Him? *Let* God have complete control?! What was I thinking? When would it dawn on me that He had already taken over, whether I agreed with it or not? So much for violating my free will, I thought. You know, I still can't find that in the Bible, that verse that implies He never violates our free will. Where exactly is that verse?

I THOUGHT BACK to the fall a year and a half earlier as I drove east from Lewiston, Idaho, toward Sheridan, having just received the check for my share of the business I had co-owned and sold. I complained to God about losing my family.

"You have a new family now," He said, *"one that will never leave you."*

"Okay, I guess. Thanks, sort of," I answered. Actually, I wanted mine back, but then I realized that they apparently hadn't liked me all that well. I wasn't sure how well my new family liked me either. My track record with "church people" was somewhat dismal.

Also, I wasn't so sure *I* liked my new family. A friend reminded me that you can choose your friends, but you can't choose your family. Real funny. But then, just maybe, at this time in life, I could truly sit back and see what God might do. It looked like He was running everything anyway. Perhaps all that I had to do was just wait on Him. Just wait …

I'm not a hateful person. Though I may have said the word in anger, I don't think that I've ever really hated anyone. I don't even like the word. But, waiting? I hate waiting. And I knew that there was more than simply waiting involved. I knew He always wanted, sometimes even required, my input. But what kind of input? I had prayed, fasted, waited, prayed—and nothing.

What did He want from me? What was He trying to teach me?

"Hey, Jonathan," Brad greeted me.

"Hey, Brad. What's new?"

"Not a lot. Hey, I think I made up a joke. At least I haven't heard it before. Want to hear it?"

"Tell me."

"There was this guy who developed a suicide kit with everything you need. He sold a bunch but eventually gave up, because he kept losing customers."

"I believe you made that up, Brad."

"Thanks. But you know, I get worried about you at times, bro. Should I get worried?"

"Worried? About what?"

"Oh, I was watching TV the other night, and some guy was talking about suicide, saying that people who might actually do it don't talk about it."

"And?"

"Well, you don't ever talk about it and I know you're depressed."

"Yes?"

"You okay?"

"Brad, my friend, don't worry. I think about suicide often enough. Does that pass for talking about it?"

"You do? You wouldn't do it, would you?"

"No. It seems like murdering myself, and I'm not a murderer."

"How come you even think about it?"

"Well, I'm not sure. Maybe it's kind of like having another option. I like options, even if they're not really an option. Haven't you ever thought about committing a crime, how you would pull it off?"

"Maybe, I guess. Yeah, I've thought about how I would have done a better job when I've watched a movie about a crime, but I wouldn't actually, you know."

"I know. But I admit there were times when I was so low that I think I found some comfort in planning my own demise."

"Well, you shouldn't even be doing that, bro. You know that sin always begins with a thought."

"Sometimes it begins with a thought. But suicide can be messy if you're not careful. I'm not a messy guy."

"What do you mean?"

"You know, guns and stuff. I couldn't shoot myself. Too messy."

"What would you do?"

"I thought we weren't supposed to talk about this."

"Maybe it's good for you to talk."

"Brad, you're not thinking about it and just pumping me for information, are you? I've never heard you mention suicide either. Are you …?"

"Hey, whoa, my life is cool, bro. I would have no reason. I'm talking to *you* here. What would *you* do?"

"Well, I did think about it."

So I told him my imagined plan. Drugs seemed to be a clean, appropriately scientific way. People who knew me would expect something higher-tech, so I approached a friend. The purpose was to determine how much of a controlled substance would be required to do the job. I had no idea. Though I guess I could have looked on the Internet, that wouldn't have gotten me the required human sympathy. I had heard of people who, after swallowing a whole bottle of pills, had to have their stomachs pumped. That wouldn't do anything other than add more humiliation, which I wanted to avoid.

Ann, a nurse, and I sat together on her sofa one evening.

"So, Ann, do you see failed suicide attempts at work? You know, people who botch trying to kill themselves using drugs or something?" I asked, being appropriately evasive.

"Sure, why do you ask?"

"Just curiosity."

"Don't do it, Jonathan. You're going to be all right."

"Hey, I'm just talking here. I'm just wondering about your work, just your work."

"Drugs are a bad idea unless you really know what you're doing," she warned me.

"What do you mean?" I asked, thinking some good info was coming.

"You don't want to end up gawked."

"Gawked?"

"Yes. Staring at the ceiling with a ventilator doing your breathing for you."

"No, that would be very bad," I said, rather alarmed. Gawked? The very word jarred me into stark reality. My life was presently unpleasant to me, but there were certainly so many others whose lives were much more difficult. Life could be much, much worse.

"Would you like a glass of wine?" Ann asked.

"Sure. Thanks."

So much for suicide planning for the time being, though the technical details of such a project still held some fascination to a totally bored mind. That was a major part of the dilemma I faced as an ex-so-many-things. If idle hands tend toward mischief, what about idle minds? I was used to solving problems and planning for the future.

Now unlike Edison, I'm not good with repeated failures. A few failures are all right, but if something doesn't gel within a reasonable amount of time, I tend to lose interest. It's a problem I have with prayer—lack of persistence. I will exhaust every means and go to any length to perform on a job contract, but I get frustrated with prayer. No visible progress. I like to see evidence that I'm getting somewhere. Drilling wells is not for me. One too many dry holes, and I'm out of there. When designing machines, though I can keep a pretty complex idea in my brain during the concept phase, I like to go out and build some part of it to see it work, to touch it. For example, software engineers can run parts of their programs, which is good.

Then there's civil engineering—a different kind of nightmare. If I make a mistake designing a machine, I can start over. But what if you move part of a mountain and then decide you've made a mistake? You can't just put a mountain back so easily.

I recall a lady who came to my house after I had logged a section of her property sometime in 1982.

"I'm going to sue you. I've locked the gate so you can't get your equipment out, and my attorney will be calling you," she threatened.

"Why are you going to sue me?" I pictured her five-dollar lock on their thirty-dollar gate keeping my ten-ton logging Caterpillar from finding its way to freedom as I sat on top, "unable" to stop the machine from simply driving over her little gate and reducing it to thirty cents' worth of scrap iron.

"Because, you cut down the trees in my favorite place," she cried. "I've been going there since I was a child. You *ruined* it."

Ruined it? Was turning a bunch of over-ripe, matured-out, rotting, white fir trees into useful pulpwood ruining something? Did she expect to make no sacrifice for the right to read her daily newspaper? Were we supposed to "ruin" other people's property instead? I was reminded of my hip friends who hated the loggers, but loved their wooden houses, or others who saw messes as only belonging in others' backyards. "Ma'am, your husband had a timber expert come in and mark the trees I was supposed to cut according to our contract. I cut them down and hauled the logs to the mill. Getting an attorney is a waste of money. I have the contract," I said.

She got pretty hysterical and continued to argue, until I actually had to explain to her that I could not put the trees back, which is what she really wanted. I assured her that after I piled the brush, seeded the ground and a hundred or so years had passed, it would actually look pretty nice. Now, I am lying. I would never say anything like that to anyone—which might be a bit of a lie too. Anyway, she finally left. I thought briefly about calling ahead and warning her husband to seek shelter, but I didn't like him that much.

Failures and planning. No, I was not used to repeated failures, which interfere with planning. Planning assumes a degree of success. Success eluded me and I was losing confidence. I began to dislike looking at the future and was running out of stuff to even think about. What was I supposed to do with my mind?

THE GLASS OF wine. Ann taught me about decent wine, red wine, which is supposed to be good for you or something. Though I was never very fond of alcohol, I had experimented with drugs years ago. Being high may have had some value as recreation, but I had always preferred keeping a clear mind. Alcohol was common around our house when I was growing up, but I never developed a taste for hard liquor. Not that I didn't try. I did want to fit in, so I pretended to enjoy the stuff, when necessary, to make an appropriate impression. I do understand that people pay good money for Scotch and bourbon, but not me. And I had never learned much about wines. What little I did drink came mostly from boxes, which fit the refrigerator better than those round bottles with the meaningless names.

But a few weeks after Cathie left, I did have a brief encounter with hard stuff. I decided to drown my sorrows in booze. I didn't know much about what to buy, so I visited my friends at the local state liquor store.

"Hi, Wendy."

"Hi, Jonathan. You looking for Arnie? He's not here."

"Nope, I'm looking for something to drink."

"You? I didn't think you drank. You serious?"

"Yeah, I want to get drunk. I remember not liking Scotch or bourbon much. What tastes good? Do you have any suggestions?"

"You are serious."

"I am."

"Is that a good idea? I mean, are you okay?" Everybody in town knew.

"No. I'm not okay. That's why I want to drink. Suggest something."

"Okay. Well, here's what a lot of guys buy."

"I'll take it. Thanks, Wendy."

"Sure. Hope you feel better. Might be smart to pick up some aspirin too."

"Thanks. I have some."

I took the bottle home, poured some of it into a glass with plenty of ice, took a big swig and immediately gagged. It was awful. "Why do people drink this stuff?" I wondered. This wasn't going to work without a lot of effort. Eventually I found that by holding my nose, I could get enough down to manage a pretty good drunk. The first evening, I amused myself by playing the piano and then fell asleep. It seemed like a decent way to avoid the pain, so I drank the remainder the next evening.

I was in the habit of running six miles every other day, and the following day was a run day. Running was not something I actually enjoyed, but it was a great stress reliever. At that time, stress was available in spades. Our business, a machining and fabricating job shop, was extremely busy. I had three custom machines to design for customers, several of our production machines were partially down and I was being divorced. Though I'd heard that some people experience dysfunction during the stress of divorce, I just wanted to be busy doing something. Running was another thing that I could do to pass time. Passing time, I was sure, would eventually lessen the awful pain that had become a persistent background noise darkening my soul. Activity covered up that noise, though only temporarily.

But then, that day, as I rounded the end of my driveway and headed down the road to begin my run, I distinctly heard these words, *"Lose the alcohol."*

That was all. Seemed like a strange way for God to address me, not very friendly at all. People use the term *tone of voice* which is the best I can come up with to describe the inflection, which is sometimes, though not always, evident when He speaks. Some say that God speaks to us in the same words that we would use. That could be. Maybe that was it. Though it might be the way I would address my son, if I had one, it still did not sound very kind.

So I did not drink a drop of alcohol until I was having dinner with Gary and his wife in Denver eight months later and was offered a glass of wine. Was it okay to have a little wine? Even then, as I took a sip, I wondered if God was displeased. It had been a long time since He had told me not to drink, and maybe it was just hard alcohol He was concerned about. Maybe beer or wine, diluted alcohol, would be okay.

SIN IS FUNNY that way. There is an obvious direct commandment to cease something, and there I was, thinking that a diluted form of the same thing might be acceptable. Where else could I apply that principle? What could I, in my own life, find acceptable in diluted form that would be untouchable full strength? Lying? Stealing? Pride? Idolatry?

I do have a basic doctrinal position on sin with which I am sufficiently comfortable to keep me from drowning in guilt and doubt. The position resulted from a mix of solid teaching, Bible study and another brief conversation with God.

It was probably 1982 and I was driving my log truck up a narrow, bumpy road that led to decks, or piles, of prime Ponderosa pine logs on a remote piece of private property east of Riggins, Idaho. As I was being tossed around in the truck, my temper rose with each thrust from the rocks and ruts. Though I had enjoyed parts of logging and hauling, the jostling was getting harder to take, possibly because I was getting older? I started cursing, but immediately caught myself and repented. Then I felt weak. Being very perfect was important. I took a lot of pride in my walk with the Lord, and probably held some contempt for others who could not live up to my standards.

"Am I ever going to overcome this anger, Lord? I'm so sick of it. I'm such a fair-weather Christian. Please deliver me from this stupid anger. I'm so sorry about it."

"I'm not bothered by your anger."

He was there, speaking quite clearly again, not while I was on my knees, not in church, but there in my truck on this bumpy, dusty, lonely back-Idaho road where I was making a bare living and getting frustrated with it.

"But I'm sinning. I hate myself for sinning. I can't seem to stop doing some things. I'm getting nowhere."

"You're doing fine."

"But I'm not fine. My sinning is a constant problem."

"It's not a problem to Me. My Son died for your sins, all of them. Your sins are a problem to you, not to Me."

I had to ponder those words for a long time, eventually for years, so any reasonable response was impossible. Why it was and is sometimes still so difficult for me to grasp the fact that I'm okay with God remains a mystery. Some folks are able to accept His divine gift without question or doubt. Perhaps, for me, it just feels too easy and I have some deeply ingrained need to work for everything. But that feeling may not be all bad, for I do not take His gift for granted.

But the implication of His words was huge. What was the point of struggling against sin if God seemed to be okay with it? First, God was not actually saying that He was totally okay with my situation. He said that it was not a problem to *Him* but to *me*. Though He disapproved of my sinning, He had made provision for it, and the package was complete. I could not add anything to that package. In spite of all of the talk about grace, avoiding even the appearance of sin was central to most of the preaching and teaching I'd heard. So what was I trying to do?

It was probably then that the mysterious talked-about-but-never-attained standards of righteousness began to catch my attention.

DIFFERENT CHURCHES AND denominations have different standards. Some allow alcohol; some don't. Dancing is of the devil for some, while for others, you practically need to dance to be saved. Then there's the tongues dilemma. These are the obvious, acknowledged standards which often cause sufficient friction between believers to break down communication. We seem more concerned about the emphasis on external cleanliness, the tendency to rely on the ornamentation of degrees and accomplishments, and the conforming to ritual or accepted behavior as a means of identifying those who are walking in a manner pleasing to God, rather than by their spirit.

1 Corinthians 2:13–15 says, "But a natural man does not accept the things of the Spirit of God; for they are foolishness to him, and he cannot understand them, because they are spiritually appraised. But he who is spiritual appraises all things, yet he himself is appraised by no man."

Appraised by no man? If I was to be appraised by no man, how was I supposed to know how I was doing? I had no scorecard from God. He had said that my sin was not a problem to Him, but to me. Were we not admonished to warn a brother if we see him sinning? What was the point of admonishing if God didn't care? But God does care. Why? What problem could my sin be to me if God has forgiven all of them?

I know the simple answers to these questions. I'm not ignorant of Bible teaching, but to give a simple answer to a question is to assume that the question is simple. I don't think that these are truly simple questions. The questions are *basic, but not simple*. There are more than a few ways that these questions are answered, which is evidence that thoughtful people have struggled over them. And that's okay. It isn't necessary to have complete answers even for basic questions.

The words *I don't know* are seldom heard from pulpits in churches I've attended. Yet there is so much about God that we do not know. That's okay, too. If Paul rightly declares that we see through a glass darkly, how can *we* claim to see much at all? The outpouring by the Lord of an abundance of revelation in the latter part of the twentieth century was certainly a blessing, but the fallout has been the precipitation of idolatrous ministries and churches proclaiming salvation from discomfort by adhering to their specific formulae for Christian living. Knowledge flourished and divisions arose. The abundance of knowledge only seemed to create more division, more answers to what seemed like basic, simple questions.

Jesus died for every sin ever committed. If we ask, forgiveness is granted—provided we forgive, an interesting and often ignored condition. But our sins can still be a serious problem to us.

EACH DAY, THOUGH I was learning how little I really understood about God, I was gaining some new insight into what the real consequences of sin might be and how He viewed my situation. I was sitting on the edge of my bed in the early spring of 2004. Sitting, praying and thinking—grumbling.

"You have it backwards. You assume that because you suffer, I've rejected you," He said suddenly.

"Yes," I agreed, perking somewhat up, as I had been feeding my depression and expressing myself; which, viewed by someone else, might be called whining.

The very clear and precise voice came from a few feet to my left front, at about my level. "Yes, that's right. Now we're making some sense here," I mumbled to myself. Finally, God was coming around to my way of thinking, I reckoned. If you want someone to go away, treat them badly long enough and they will leave. It was rejection, plain and simple. What could be more obvious?

"No. You have it backwards," He repeated. *"It's an honor to suffer for Me."*

Some people might think that I make this up. But I don't come up with this kind of stuff. Absolutely not. God always has a different viewpoint, a higher realm of thinking that catches me totally unaware. His few simple words expand into a vast new perspective on situations. Yes, of course. Suffering is an honor. I knew that. Duh. It's all through the Bible. Apparently, I needed reminding. To do anything for Him is an honor.

So how come I was whining? Probably because I don't like to suffer. Does anybody?

The next morning as I walked into our office, Lori, our office manager, said, "Hi, Jonathan. And how are you today?"

Lori's a gem. God strategically surrounded me with all kinds of people. I've often complained to Him that I seldom feel His love. I've even accused Him of not loving me, yet He was always loving me through the people He surrounded me with. Lori was one. Though I often listened to the story of her difficult divorce, she listened more to me. I'm grateful for knowing her.

"Well?" she asked again.

I said, after thinking for a moment, "I'm honored."

"What? What did you say? Honored?" she asked with delightful curiosity.

"Yeah. God told me that it was an honor to suffer for Him."

"Wow! Did He really? Did He really say that?"

"Yeah. Yesterday. While I was praying, or more precisely, whining."

"Wow. Cool. Did He say anything else?"

"Yeah. He said, 'You have it backwards. You assume that because you suffer, I've rejected you.' I agreed. I thought that He was starting to see my point. But he continued, 'No. You have it backwards. It's an honor to suffer for Me.'"

"Yeah. Cool. That sounds like Him, something He would say. So do you feel better?"

"Better? Well, I'm not sure. I guess I should feel better. It was pretty neat, though, you know? I mean, there I am sitting on my bed and bang, there He was. The words were clear as a bell. No mistaking."

"Really cool! So should we call you Mr. Honored or something? Hi, Mr. Honored. It sure is an honor to be honored by Mr. Honored's honored presence. Ha-ha!"

"Great, Lori. Really nice. You should be more reverent. We're talking about the Lord here, you know? Come on."

"Me? Me? Hey, Mr. Honored, you should talk! You're like the loose goose with the reverence thing. Don't lay that on me, oh honored one. Reverence? Sure."

"Okay, okay. Enough with the grief. Did we get any money in here?"

"I haven't checked the mail yet. Make yourself useful. Go check the mail."

"I can do that," I said, and walked out to the mailbox and returned with the pile. As I sorted through the envelopes, I griped, "No money, again! Doesn't anybody feel like taking a few minutes to write us a simple check?! Do our customers think we're running a charity shop or something? What'er we here for anyway?!"

"To suffer," Lori answered gently.

"Suffer ... right. I forgot already."

AND THINGS ARE backwards in this world. The last shall be first. The bottom shall be the top. The back shall be the front. The floor shall be the ceiling. Apparent rejection is honored acceptance. I wanted God to love me directly, one on one, but He liked loving me through all sorts of different people with all kinds of problems and issues.

Yes, we do have so much backwards. The more knowledge and understanding we claim to have, the less we truly have of God. Knowledge and understanding are good, but they quickly become idols as soon as we place much trust in their correctness. I had never been comfortable with the teaching I had heard on suffering. Now, it was apparently an honor to suffer for Him. If so, why are we quick to treat those who are suffering as someone in need of correction or fixing? Does God do better work through damaged lives? Could knowledge, improperly used, actually be a detriment?

So much to think about. New things. I thought I needed fixing. All the counseling, divorce care classes, teaching and preaching I heard supported that. Now I wasn't so sure. Maybe I was in better shape than I'd been led to believe.

7

Number Two

Sometimes we need to just stand back and say to our self,
"Self? Doggone it, self!"

ANOTHER LIGHT WAS there on the horizon. This would be a real fire with some serious warmth. It would, however, require a lot of fuel, get out of control, burn me, and cause more loss.

"God told me to come here and tell you that He has sent His Holy Spirit out to find your Rebekah."

"Excuse me?"

It was early in December 2003, and I was sitting alone on a Wednesday evening at a church. I was waiting for some single men to show up for fellowship. It was a pointless wait, for no one was coming. Why would they? There were no women. Many churches separate single men and women in evening meetings. Too dangerous, they think. Might turn into a "dating service" and spoil their fine name. We can't be trusted together.

I promised no ax grinding, so enough said. I had somehow been appointed to facilitate the male side of the singles ministry at this particular church. How I got to be the facilitator or leader is not clear to me now, though it may have made some sense at the time. There I was, and this guy walked in.

"God told me to tell you that He has sent His Holy Spirit out to find your Rebekah," he repeated.

"Really?"

"Yep."

"Who are you?"

"Devin. Would you like to hear my story about how God brought me my wife?"

"You're married?"

"Yep."

"You're not allowed in here. This is a church-sanctioned meeting for singles, which you are not."

"Are you asking me to leave? It doesn't look very well attended. Do you want to just sit here alone? My story is good."

He was right. I was bored stiff. A visit from a Martian would have been welcome. "I'm listening," I said.

"Good. You see, God showed me my next wife while I was still married to my first wife. I couldn't believe it," he said.

"I can imagine. Did you arrive here in a car or a spaceship?" I asked, thinking I had my Martian.

"I don't own a spaceship. Look, this sounds incredible, I know, but I'm convinced God wants me to tell you this story. He knows what he's doing, so you could at least listen."

I supposed that by saying that *God knows what He is doing*, Devin was intending to throw me off track and convince me that he had some connection with reality. I didn't buy it for a minute. But his effort was worth some reward, and he might be entertaining.

"Go on," I sighed. "I'm sure I haven't heard this before."

Devin went on to tell me a one-of-a-kind story about being in a miserable marriage and having God show him another woman to whom he has been married for many years. He has had some remarkable experiences with God, but that's *his* story to tell.

THE FOLLOWING SPRING, a friend suggested I contact on out-of-state woman. "I think it's the Lord," he said. I know this man. He would not say such a thing lightly, so I called her. It was electrifying. We connected so well that I made plans to drive to meet her within a few days.

I want to make something clear. I am not an impulsive person. Decisions driven by emotion, pure speculation, perceived threat or intimidation are not part of my behavior. At least they weren't until then. What followed was out of character for me. I was about to violate my historical standards of behavior and act like a love-crazed madman.

I asked her to marry me the day after meeting her. It seemed so strange. Were these words coming from my lips? She knew nothing of Devin's tale concerning a Rebekah, told to me three months earlier, yet she said to me, "The morning you arrived, just before you came to my door, the Lord told me I was a Rebekah." Maybe I was a madman, but I was one smitten madman. Had my nightmare finally come to an end?

MARRIAGE IS SOMEWHAT like life on an island. You are flying along in your life with many degrees of freedom, and then you're married. Your freedom is restricted. Though actually very useful, some people are not able to adjust to such a restriction. Marriage is bondage to them.

In God's kingdom, perceived restrictions are actually liberating. It is another backwards kingdom principle. Properly connected and fitted into place, we can grow, blossom, and produce joyful fruit accompanied by peace and contentment. Not many find that true connection. Those that fail remain like individual plants in a garden made for a single Vine. They see the Vine, talk about the Vine, admire the Vine, give apparent worship to the Vine, and try to be like the Vine in every way. Those actually connected to the Vine are often invisible to the unconnected individuals, being so well-blended into the Vine that they appear either inconsequential or as some alien life form. Alien because they represent a part of the Vine having an unfamiliar function or appearance. If the observers were really a part of the Vine, they would recognize the Vine's other parts, though they still may have to look around a bit.

As for me, I enjoyed married life. I wanted to be married again, and now I thought I saw another soul well connected to the Vine. The emotional, spiritual and physical attractions were intense. Had I really asked her to marry me, a woman I hardly knew? Who was I anymore? Nobody I knew.

Now, for a few days it seemed that my historical self was resurfacing quickly enough to abort a possible landing on a truly unknown island. We had intended to live in the same town for a while and possibly get married at some later date. It appeared that we were back in the cool, calm air where we could see clearly enough to make our own plans. The landing into a quick marriage would be avoided. But *apparently* God wanted to keep things moving along. The aborted landing turned into only a change in approach, and, through a series of very strange events, we were soon married. It didn't last long.

There is little that is relevant or appropriate to write about concerning my second marriage. But there was a purpose in that marriage which I've come to understand, accept and am trying to appreciate. We were married for around five months, and then it was over. Some of the things the Lord has talked to me about I could not understand without the benefit of both marriages—especially the second one. I believe that it is consistent with Biblical teaching that there are roads which God leads some down to teach them things, to allow them the honor of experiencing Him in a unique way, to glorify Himself, to chasten, or to send a message to others.

I realize the idea that God would direct someone to enter into a doomed relationship seems highly suspect, and there is probably reason to suppose that the marriage was not actually destined for failure. I understand the difficulty of accepting that it was God's direction. That's okay. I believed it was God's direction; I made the decision and I'm responsible.

The concept of shared responsibility can be illusive. We cannot be responsible for doing what is improper, for sinning, and not take responsibility for doing what is proper. That is, as we decide to sin we also decide to do what is right. Though God has, on occasion, given me explicit instructions which I feel an undeniable compulsion to perform, choices are the norm. Sometimes I know my next destination, but often I have only a clear first step. Sometimes there is nothing.

SOMETIME IN THE summer of 2004, while I was married to my second wife, the Lord spoke to me on two separate occasions as I was showering. He does that often, talks to me while I am showering.

"This is not about you and (your wife). This is about Me, and I will prevail," the Lord said.

I have some explanations for this statement, but I would rather let the rest of my experiences speak along with these words from God. The implication is that there is something larger to be grasped than a simple marriage between two people.

"This is not about gratification or short-term satisfaction. This is about long-term peace and contentment," He said a few weeks later.

The obvious explanation for this statement is that the marriage was not for sexual or emotional gratification, nor was it a band-aid to sooth my loneliness and desire for companionship. The experience of the marriage was to contribute somehow to my long-term well being. I believe it will. Though my credibility took a serious hit, I try to be grateful for the experience.

I also had five significant dreams during the marriage, and some intense interaction with the Lord. The dreams, though they seemed to relate to my marriage, seemed also to represent aspects of the relationship between Jesus and His church. Certainly, marriage is a type of mini church, so it is not unusual for the Lord to teach us through our marriage relationships.

Some of the substance of the above experiences is addressed indirectly later in observations about the church as it is today.

AND I STILL had my friends. Was it Gandhi that said he had no problem with Jesus, but that it was His followers he disliked? I didn't *dislike* Brad, though I didn't really *like* him either. He was just there.

"Hey, Jonathan."
"Hey, Brad."
"You doin' okay?"
"I'm okay, sure."
"You don't sound okay."
"I'm okay, okay?"
"You're not okay, bro. I can tell."
"I'm fine, okay? How are *you*? How's your wife? Kids?"
"They're fine. Thanks for asking. We're doing a remodel and I know that I'm going to need lots of prayer to get through it. Man! I don't know why we do these things sometimes. I guess she'll be happy when we're done."

"She's not happy now?"

"Of course she is! I didn't mean anything like that. She's happy, man! Things are good. I bought her a new TV, and we're making a great room where we can all watch it together. She's way happy. I mean it, really."

"Okay, okay, I believe that you believe she's happy. Good deal."

"Yeah … just walking the walk, me and my wife, keeping our eyes on Jesus. Just like when Peter got out of the boat, you know. Do you remember that? When Peter got out of the boat and almost sank because he took his eyes off Jesus? You know that scripture? Where is that? John?"

"I think maybe it's in Matthew."

"Matthew? Sounds like something that should be in John. But it could be Matthew. Anyway, that's what you need to do, keep your eyes on Jesus. Don't pay any attention to those things that aren't going right. That's what got Peter. He took his eyes off Jesus."

"Fine, Brad. Thanks a bunch."

"Are you hearing me, bro? It is the answer here."

"I know the scripture and I know that interpretation, which I don't actually agree with. Jesus didn't admonish Peter for taking his eyes off Him or for looking at the circumstances. He said he had little faith and questioned why he doubted. Thank you for bringing it up, I guess."

"There you go again."

"What?"

"You know. You question everything. People think that you think you know everything."

"Just because I question things, I'm accused of being a know-it-all?"

"Well, kind of, yeah. It's just that every time people come to help you, give you a scripture or something, you act like you've heard it all before. You know? Like nobody has anything new."

"Every time?"

"Well, yeah. Most times."

"Yikes, Brad! Come on. I *have* read the Bible through like four times probably, and taught Bible studies for years. I know a few things. Is there some problem with having some knowledge? Do I have to play dumb just so you can feel that you've done your daily good deed and been an encourager? Should I do that for you? Would that make you feel better?"

"You know …? You don't really have to do anything for me. I'm just trying to help. It was just a suggestion. Forget about it."

"What? What's the suggestion?"

"Keeping your eyes on Jesus, man. It's the answer."

"Okay, Brad, would you really like to help me? Would you really?"

"Sure, buddy, anything. What do you need? I'm here for you. What can I do?"

"Point Him out to me."

"What?"

"Point Jesus out to me!"

"What are you talking about?"

"Look, lately I can't see Him. So point Him out to me. Where is He? I mean, He was standing right there in front of Peter. That was easy. You're walking this eyes-on-Jesus thing so well. Help me here. Point Him out to me so I can keep my eyes on Him. I promise; once I find Him, I won't let Him out of my sight."

"Ha! That's good. You know, you are a piece of work. I love you, man. I really do. You are funny. You just about had me. I thought you were serious."

"I am."

"Sure. Hey, look, it's been great, but I've got a few things to do. You take care, brother, and remember."

"What?"

"Eyes, man, eyes. You know where."

"Thanks for the help, Brad."

"Hey, anytime. An-ee-time. Don't be a stranger. Call me. Anytime."

"Sure. You'll be the first one."

"Sounds like a plan, bro. Love ya."

8

Clarity

Enough with the labor pains. Show me the baby.

I'VE ALWAYS WANTED to live in the West. I like the clarity. With few exceptions, the rest of my relatives have stayed near the East Coast, so my western-life affection is probably not due to genetics. Though I grew up in the East, something compelled me to head west. Perhaps I just wanted out, to be away from all the people. The West owns those clear skies and huge vistas where you can see for miles. Nothing is hidden from view by thousands of trees like in the East. When we returned to Baltimore in 1986, my daughter Anna had remarked that someone needed to cut down a bunch of the trees so people could see where they were. She noticed the difference immediately.

In the West, the night sky is a three-dimensional spray of stars floating in an inky black void that stretches to infinity. As I appreciate some graphic arts displays where objects are exact, set against a sharply contrasting background and severely delineated from each other, I appreciate clearness and high-definition. If there is a problem, what is the exact problem? Let's get some clarity going, and we can deal with things. Some folks prefer a sort of gray, fuzzy environment, where issues are not well-defined. It's as if they prefer an available quick getaway or a lack of true accountability. I like to ask, *Exactly what did you mean when you said such and such?* Tell it straight. Enough with the sizzle, show me the steak.

IT WAS SOMETIME IN 1988 that I flew from Baltimore to the airport outside Helena, Montana. Someone was supposed to pick me up at the airport and take me to a motel. It was a small airport and mine was the last plane arriving for the day, so they closed the airport. Everyone left. I was standing alone in front of the small terminal building. I mean, *everyone* else was gone.

How quiet it was! The Big Sky country of Montana was laid out before me. It was true, I thought. The sky really did seem much bigger here. It was so quiet. Absolute, delicious silence, so unlike the East, where noise is constant.

There wasn't a sound until, suddenly, a meadowlark sang out off in the distance. There is clarity, I thought. There is delineation. Nothing gray here. The sound of the meadowlark was clear and bright against total silence. He sang again and again. Scrumptious. Me, the meadowlark, and the high desert. Nice. I literally tasted the simplicity.

After a while, I heard a car in the distance, and in several minutes some dust was visible. Then finally, yes, it was a car arriving with a great noise that ended the delightful experience.

"You must be Jonathan."
"I am."
"Hop in."
"Thanks."

It would be nice if God spoke to us clearly—as clearly as the meadowlark. *Sometimes* He does.

IT WAS PROBABLY in the fall of 2004. The night was cool and clear and I was driving west along Route 200 in Montana, alone, about eighty miles from the Idaho border. I was divorced for a second time, humiliated, business was not going well and another fire had gone out.

"You're upset."
"Yes, I'm upset."
"You're upset with Me."
"Uh, You? I uh …"

It was apparent that a conversation with God was going on. I didn't realize it at first, but the thoughts in my mind were not all mine. Though I had been mulling over my situation as I drove, Someone had joined in.

CONVERSATIONS WITH GOD come in many different forms. I have often asked people if God speaks to them. Most replies are vague.

"Well, you know. He speaks to me through the sunset or the flowers or something."

"Yeah, that's nice, but has He ever said something to you that you could write down, that you could repeat verbatim?"

"Well, I don't really know. I'm not sure. I can't remember."

"Not sure? Do you mean to tell me that you're not sure or can't remember if God spoke to you? *God*?"

"I'm not sure. He may have."

"Has your *mother* spoken to you?"

"Of course."

"Dad?"

"Come on. Look, I think maybe God has spoken to me, or at least I assume that He has spoken to me, but I can't remember anything that I could write down. Okay?"

"Would you like Him to say something that you could write down? We could pray right now that He would speak to you plainly about something."

"Well … I don't know. I guess that would depend."

"Depend? Depend on what?"

"Depend on what He would say."

Depend on what He would say? Amazing. Could it be that we don't hear from God because we don't want to hear what He has to say? Does God have specific things to say to us individually that we should be able to write down? Are we selective in our hearing? That is, do we hear only what we want to hear? What does Matthew 13:9 mean? "He who has ears, let him hear." Do we all have ears? Can we pray for ears?

There is another conversation I've had a few times, which is a variation of the above.

"If God asked you to do something, would you do it?" I've asked.

"Well, yes. Of course."

"*Well,* yes? What's that mean?"

"Well, I guess, depending on what He asked, I guess. I mean, if I knew it was Him. You know."

"Suppose you knew it was Him. Would you do whatever He asked, no matter what it was?"

"How would I know it was Him?"

"That's a given. If somehow you were *absolutely positive* it was God, would you do whatever He asked you to do?"

"Well, I don't know how I would be absolutely positive that it was God."

Is this evasive? Ideally our position should be one of complete obedience. The criteria for determining whether or not it is God doing the asking should not be a set of standards, a sort of filter He must pass through, but simply the knowledge of Him and His voice. Is not God large enough to handle our mistaking someone else for Him, some other voice, in our intention of pleasing Him? Would He not be more pleased with our sincere attempt to be immediately responsive to His desires than with our trying to find every reason why it may not be Him doing the asking?

God is well able to be trusted with our errors, especially those made in honest attempts to seek His will. If *love covers a multitude of sins* is valid, is not truly acting in love sufficient to cover what might be error or perceived as error?

During the spring of 2002, while I was hanging around waiting to see what would become of my divorce, I met Wednesday mornings with a small group of men. Though we pretended to have a Bible study, we really met for mutual encouragement. The group was eclectic. There were a couple of battle-weary pastors, a few young men, a scripture memory-master, a fundamentalist suffering from advanced ALS (Lou Gehrig's disease), a staunch Baptist, and me.

Several of us had quarreled years before, sometimes bitterly. Churches had split, words had been said, offenses taken, and some of these guys were left to pick up the pieces left by the damage caused by others who had moved on.

As I sat with them one day, I had an inspiration or mental picture of the Lord clarifying some information He had begun transmitting years ago. It was another template with parts missing that He placed in my mind and filled in over the years. A picture gradually formed. I do not claim what follows to be a prophecy of any kind. It simply seems to sit well within what I believe God has shown me.

I voiced my thoughts to the men, "The next movement will be the love movement. We've seen supernatural gifts, knowledge and independent fellowships, but in the next movement, all of the divisions will be irrelevant. There will be a group of people who will unite in their love for God and for each other. Their love for each other and devotion to Him alone will astonish the world."

MY CONVERSATIONS WITH God vary from vague impressions about what He might be implying to exact words that hang like sparkling crystals in the air and remain etched indelibly into my memory, available for instant recall, lest I forget. The following experience was not a clear, verbal exchange. The thoughts were real-time information placed in my mind which I converted into words so that I could respond.

Sometimes He seems removed from me, a few feet off to the left or right. This time, He was definitely right in my head—or probably right in my face.

"You're upset with Me."

"Okay, I'm upset with You, but that doesn't sound good when I say it. Something's wrong with that … I'm thinking." I was thinking.

"Good. Think about this too. Think of another word."

"Another word?"

"Yes, another word."

"Uh, still thinking."

"I'll help you. You're _____ in Me. You fill in the blank."

"Hmmm."

"Think about how you feel."

"This is very bad."

"Go ahead."

"Disappointed."

"Bingo. Now say it all. Say the whole sentence."

"I'm disappointed in You. That sounds bad. Yeah, that's not good."

"My, you're doing so well here. Disappointed? Now, why are you, man, disappointed in Me, God?"

"Well, You know."

"Sure, I know. I know everything. It's one of the advantages of being

God, but I want to hear it from you."

"Why? Why would you want to hear it from me?"

"So you can hear what it sounds like."

"It sounds very bad when I say it."

"But you're thinking it. You say you're big on this clarity stuff. Steak and sizzle and all that. Saying things clarifies your position to you and to others. Go ahead then and say what you are thinking."

"Well, You're not doing what You're supposed to be doing."

"I'm not?" He replied.

"I know these are the wrong answers, but no, you're not—I guess."

"According to whom?"

"I guess, me. Sounds pretty dumb, huh?"

"You're the one with the opinions, making the judgments here."

Now I was cringing. I felt like crawling under the seat.

"So what am I supposed to be doing that I'm failing to do?" He inquired.

"Well, You know."

"Say it, Jonathan."

"Making things work out."

"Good. Now, is that part of my job, to make things go your way, to make everything work out for your benefit?"

"Well, probably not. A lot of people say that though. You know they do. I guess I kind of knew that was not really true even though I liked the idea, and it seemed to be working."

"It did work for a while, and you found that I can do amazing things. But you knew that there was more."

"Yes, I did, but I guess I forgot. I got on with my life and sort of forgot about you in many ways. It was wrong."

"Then, what's the problem?"

"I'm sure it's me."

"Go on."

"Well, I guess I've been expecting that, at least after some reasonable time, You would make things work out. Sort of like You used to."

"So what needs to change here?"

"I guess my expectations."

"Good. You're learning quickly."

"It doesn't seem *quickly*. Things haven't gone well for a long time. Seems like forever."

"Do you still trust Me, Jonathan?"

"But absolutely nothing is going right."

"Do you trust me?"

"I'm not sure what to trust You for anymore. What can I expect?"

"Do you trust me?"

"I trust you to be God, but I don't even know what that means anymore. I used to know, but I have no idea anymore."

I remembered a man once saying to me, "Your expectations are the source of your frustrations. You expect and you don't get. That can be frustrating." So now I wondered if I should quit expecting. What about my hopes and dreams, or my plans? How do they fit in with my expectations?

Lesson one—unconditional trust.

FRANK WAS A solid guy who would not hesitate to speak frankly with me.

"Frank?"

"What?"

"God is not who I'm thinking he is."

"Splendid. Wait while I turn on my recorder. I want to play this back for you so you'll learn to be more careful about what you say."

"Funny. I didn't know you had a sense of humor."

"Who's being funny?"

"Listen, as a child you idolized your parents, right?"

"Most people do."

"Then you grew up, or most people do."

"Great observation."

"So your perceptions changed," I added.

"Yeah. I saw them as imperfect people who made mistakes. Most rational people transition from an idealized, childish picture of life to reality. A good, complete transition allows for forgiveness and acceptance of life as it really is. You know this. For lots of reasons, many are slow to make a complete transition. Some never do."

"Could this same process happen in our relationship with God?" I asked. "I'm not saying that we find out He is imperfect. But could we have childish expectations which we need to get over? Paul said in 1 Corinthians 13:11–12, 'When I was a child, I used to speak as a child, think as a child, reason as a child; when I became a man, I did away with childish things.'"

"Wasn't Paul talking about spiritual gifts?" Frank questioned.

"Maybe, but what if he was thinking about a better way of seeing God, a more mature way? Maybe he was pointing to the future, but why could we not try to see a different way now? Maybe we have made our dark glass darker ourselves. Let me give you an example. Would God cause a divorce?"

"God hates divorce," Frank reminded me.

"Do you think He would hate seeing someone slashed open with a knife?"

"Of course."

"What if they had cancer?"

"What do you mean?"

"How do you think a child would feel seeing her mother being cut open with a knife?" I proposed.

"So her mother is being operated on for cancer. Okay. Divorce is not an operation for cancer. You can't just draw random parallels. You're always trying to do that."

"Always?"

"Lots of times."

"You know, someone said that words like *always, never* and *everything* should be removed from our language. After all, we're becoming a nation that loathes absolutes. People are always using them," I remarked.

"You just did."

"There are always exceptions. The exception makes the rule, you know."

"What does that mean?"

"I haven't a clue," I admitted.

"Look, you can't question everything, Jonathan. You need to accept that *some* things about God are accepted by most Christians."

"I don't question everything. I accept things."

"Name one."

"Give me a break, Frank. I'm just questioning some basic beliefs. I often feel like I have to choose between some dearly held fundamental teaching or the One whom I see as God. There are inconsistencies that I can't rectify."

"Could just be your perceptions," Frank said.

"I'm not dealing with mere perceptions. Stuff has happened. Events have taken place. These events are not coincidental. I can look back at a long series of documented events that simply defy natural progression. It had to be God all the way. Then He speaks to me, apparently challenging me to accept His being behind it all. I have to change my perception of Him to accept what He presents to me. I have to choose between what I hear and experience and much of what I hear being taught."

"I guess you have to go with what you believe to be Him."

"So He wouldn't cause a divorce?" I asked.

"No. Why would He? The Bible even says, 'Whatever God has joined together, let no man separate.'"

"What if He hadn't joined them together in the first place? What if they just decided to get married, and God had nothing to do with it? Is that possible?"

"Accept it, brother. God did not cause your divorce. It happened."

"I know. I'm responsible. But can't I try to find some purpose here without shedding responsibility? It seems to me that there is a high level of religious correctness in our Christian lives."

"Like political correctness?" Frank asked.

"Exactly. We simply cannot deal with some issues. They're too fundamental to our faith. We're too insecure to have them challenged. You can't question a doggone thing about the Bible without hackles going up. It's like we have a religious case of OCD, obsessive-compulsive disorder. We're obsessed with external cleanliness, ritual, order and control. I have some very fundamental questions, but I feel like I have to accept traditional answers, and I can't. I believe that God might do anything.

"He commanded Abraham to sacrifice His son. What an appalling thing to ask! It's barbaric, but it's right there in the Bible. It's like we've domesticated or bridled God into someone more reasonable, who does reasonable things. We read the Bible and generate a set of conditions that are acceptable to us. Anything that happens outside those conditions is not God. God would do these things, but He would not do those things.

"The Pharisees failed to recognize Jesus because He did not meet their expectations. What if our expectations are flawed? Could that be possible? Could we be wrong? Could all of Western Christianity come crashing down if we poke some holes in it by believing that God might do things considered totally out of character? It's the height of insecurity.

"God is extremely dangerous. He might do lots of things we regard as inconsistent with scripture. Who are we to set standards for Him? We can't limit Him to certain things. He's killed a lot of people, destroyed cities and nations, flooded the whole planet, wiped out millions. He's God! He does what He pleases regardless of what we think. So, what's a divorce or two?" I concluded.

"Interesting, when you put it that way. But maybe you're just trying to get off the hook," Frank replied.

"On or off the hook. Whatever. Why is it always necessary for us to come up with a cause and effect?"

"You're doing it by blaming God. You're saying that He caused your divorce."

"I'm not saying that He is at fault. The fault is mine. The cancer was in me. I will not deny that at all, but He may have precipitated the operation."

"The divorce."

"Exactly. There are things worse than divorce, like pride and self-righteousness. Maybe the only way that I was going to get those cut out of me was through divorce. I was pretty proud."

"I can imagine."

"Thanks."

"Sure."

"You don't have to be so agreeable."

"Look, you're telling me these things. You want me to agree or disagree?"

"I want you to agree with the right things, not everything."

"Like the carnal churches?"

"Exactly. Good. You've got my drift. Listen, Frank, I'm trying to figure out some important things. I appreciate the critique. I would like to get to the bottom of these issues. Help me here."

"I'm trying. So you think that we have placed God in a box and see events outside that box as not related to or part of God's will?"

"Yes. I think that God is much bigger or less well-defined than most churches make Him out to be. They seem to want to have an exclusive on Him, to define what is of God and what is not of God by false standards, their standards."

"So what standard are we supposed to use to determine what is of God and what is not of God?"

"No standard except Him. 'My sheep know my voice and another they will not follow.'"

"That would be mayhem."

"Not if we trained people to hear His voice. Not if the real point of instruction was to teach people how to hear the voice of their Lord, instead of hammering out a standard of morality, among other things."

"Right now, we teach them to follow a set of rules? I don't completely agree. We teach people the historical facts about the birth, death, and resurrection of Jesus and the principles that He taught, principles that were expounded upon by the apostles. These are good things to teach."

"I'm not talking completeness here. Call it a course correction or something. We need to teach such things, but there is an implied set of standards that results. We encourage seeking and listening to God, but, at the same time, define what is and what is not acceptable as being from God. It's like our experiences with God are being managed."

"How?"

"Look at all of the denominations. Look at them. Everybody claims to be right. Everybody can't be right. God is not in conflict. Either tongues is from God or it's not. Churches differ."

"Does that really matter?"

"Not that, specifically; it's just an example. You just disagreed with me about divorce. Some say that miracles have ceased. There are plenty of examples."

"But these things are not significant. You're stuck on technicalities."

"The individual distinctions aren't the point. The fact that we make these distinctions *is*. We are defining what is from God and what isn't. That's the problem. Technical or not, I see few pastors challenging their congregations to truly hear directly from God."

"You seem to have issues with churches. There are plenty of solid pastors leading solid churches."

"Yes, there are. There are certainly some, but not many. Come on, Frank, I've been around. I've traveled a lot. Good fellowships are not easy to find. Drive down any road and take a sample. Visit every church. See what you find. Besides, I'm not here to knock churches. I'm trying to see God the way He wants us to see Him."

"Okay, so few church leaders truly trust their congregations enough to allow them freedom to hear from God, *whatever* He might want to say to them. They maintain control, or keep them comfortable, or whatever, by setting certain standards. It's the standard-setting itself which is the problem, not the individual standards," Frank summed up.

"We're raising babies," I said.

"Interesting."

"So what do you think Hebrews 5:13–14 means? It says, 'For everyone who partakes only of milk is not accustomed to the word of righteousness, for he is a babe. But solid food is for the mature who, because of practice, have their senses trained to discern good and evil.'"

"Mature Christians have their senses trained by practice to know what is right and what is wrong. Okay. They know by their spiritual senses, not by all these standards."

"Right. Leaders are generally qualified by their credentials, not by their ability to discern the Lord's will. Church leaders choose those who appear qualified according to their standards, who will agree with the status quo. From our government to our businesses to our churches, people generally promote others who agree with their plans, who will promote the accepted agenda, the accepted standards. Furthering the institution becomes the purpose. Change, therefore, becomes difficult."

"It may be better to choose by lot. That's what they used to do."

"Before they had standards."

"But Paul set standards."

"Right. So he set some standards. I sometimes wonder if he would still set some of the same standards now if he saw what resulted."

"Hey, I really enjoy talking about this stuff, but, if I were you, I wouldn't write any of this down."

"I'm not planning to. You know, I think we've added a lot of our own standards and made a lot of assumptions."

"Maybe, but how do we get back to the right place? How do we determine what are God's real standards and what are assumptions?"

"Start by asking Him."

"God?"
"Who else?"
"That's a thought."

DENNIS WAS ANOTHER friend. I had many people I spent lots of time talking to about God. He was our favorite subject. Our lives were pretty simple.

"Hello, Dennis?" I asked over my cell phone.
"Jonathan. How are you?"
"Okay, I guess. You busy?"
"No, not doing anything, really. You want to get together?"
"Yeah. Would it be all right if I came over for a while?"
"Sure, sure. Come on over."
"I'll take care of a couple of things and see you in about an hour?"
"Sounds great. See you in an hour."

Dennis amazed me. He lived by himself in a little apartment with no TV and just hung out with Jesus. At least that's what he said, and I have no reason to doubt it. It's not like his life was the greatest or that he's a keeper of some big secret, but he seemed to find the peace, joy and contentment that Jesus promises if we look to Him. I couldn't seem to find those comforts, and that's the problem I'd faced for a long time. I'd tried everything I knew to find that relationship I'd observed in others.

I have another friend, whom I'll call Mary, who also has a wonderful relationship with the Lord. She says she talks to Him everyday and they carry on an almost continuous conversation. She feels His presence and finds that sufficient for her, though her life has certainly been difficult.

I have no doubt that His presence could overwhelm the discomfort of any situation. Earlier in my Christian life, I had experienced that presence many times, but His presence eluded me for the most part.

THEREFORE, I HAD put considerable effort into attempts to resolve issues which might hamper receiving God's blessings and presence. Several months of group counseling with a ministry that dealt with past wounds, generational curses and missed blessings, and a week of intensive counseling resulted in nothing perceivable to me. I had submitted to help from brothers and sisters who felt that there was a definite problem with the way I perceived God, or with my relationship with Him. I had listened to critiques and admonishments, trying always to find the defect in my perception or understanding which, if corrected, would open up the floodgates of blessing and full awareness of the love and presence of God in my life.

I was aware that I was raised in a home where *I love you* was never spoken, where no one hugged and indifference was commonly felt. I still harbored significant anger and resentment, though I had confessed, asked for forgiveness and tried to lay both down at the cross many times.

Dennis was one of the ones I thought could help me.

"Hey, Dennis."

"Come on in. Blessings. Blessings. How are you?"

"Okay, I guess."

"Are you sleeping any better?"

"I guess, but I still have a hard time in the mornings. If I think too much, I start crying. I wonder if I'll ever get my life back."

"Hey, you have things to grieve about, but it seems wrong to be depressed for so long, and you've tried all the drugs."

"Yeah, the drugs just made me nervous. I've been way down that road. I've given up on the drugs, and I don't fit most of the depressed types."

"What do you mean?"

"Well, my energy is good and I like to get out and do things, and I'm trying to make things work. I'm not apathetic."

"But you can't sleep without drugs, and you're sad."

"Yeah, I guess I'm depressed. My business partner says it's like there's a gray cloud around me. I try to force a smile, but it seems so plastic. Who wants to pretend to be happy?"

"Do you think that God wants you to be miserable?"

"No, I know better. But sometimes, yes. It sounds stupid, but I do *feel* like that at times."

"There it is."

"What?"

"That's the problem. You think that God wants you to be miserable. That's wrong. He wants you to be happy, to have joy, peace and contentment. He said He came that we might have life and have it abundantly. He said we would have His joy and peace. Do you have that?"

"No."

"Well, then there's a problem."

"But I've submitted to every conceivable ministry, been anointed many times, been prayed for, and read who knows how many books. I've fasted and asked for every kind of help I could find."

"I know, but maybe it just takes time. I went through a time when I couldn't seem to find the Lord."

"How long?"

"A few months maybe. It wasn't fun. So I have some idea here."

"A few months?! This has been over four years!"

"Yeah, but you've said He has spoken to you and that you've felt His presence at times."

"Yeah. He seems to say a lot, but it has little or nothing to do with me personally. I'm aware of Him for a moment at times, but then He's gone. It's like being teased. He gives me some phrase or concept, then that's it. I'm left with wondering about me. Don't I count? Does He hate me?"

"God doesn't hate you, Jonathan. He's not out to get you."

"It feels like He's trying to run me off, get rid of me."

"But He says some really interesting things to you. He does. Maybe you only hear what you want to hear."

"Maybe. Denial is tough. Maybe I'm in denial. It's hard to see what you can't see."

"I don't think you're in denial. You're pretty open and objective about things."

"Thanks. But what can I do? I can't seem to find anything to do in any church. It's like when I was a kid. I wasn't well liked by too many guys. I was different, I guess, different and lonely."

"You said that your relationship with your father was distant, lacking in true affection."

"Yeah. Our family was like that. Nobody said, 'I love you.' Ever.

It was just not spoken. We were well-provided for and that was good enough. I don't recall ever being hugged."

"Wow! I bet that's the problem."

"What?"

"You see God the way you saw your father."

"That's probably true. Yes, I see God very much the same way that I saw my father."

"Don't you get it?"

"What?"

"There's a connection between the way you see God and the way you saw your father. We need to break that connection."

"Dennis, we've been through that. We've prayed for all those vows and ties and everything to be broken. Man, I've been through counseling, several seminars and been ministered to tons on that. Nothing changed. Nothing. What else is there to do? Maybe God just doesn't want to let me be aware of Him right now. If He wants to hide, who can find Him?"

"Why would He want to hide from you? That makes no sense. Jesus is your Lord. He takes care of you. Why would a shepherd hide from his sheep? That sure seems dumb. He said He would never leave us or forsake us. Hiding makes no sense. Our walk is a relationship. It's not one-sided. We relate to God, and He relates to us. There has to be something wrong with your relationship with Him or with the way you perceive Him."

"Yeah. Unlike me, you seem to get answers when you ask Him. I've asked Him so many times and it's only silence. You seem to simply ask Him and He answers."

"Yeah. Maybe because I listen. Maybe you're not listening."

"But He speaks to me. I've told you things He's said. That's Him. I know His voice."

"Yeah, you're right. The stuff you've told me; you definitely hear from Him. No doubt," Dennis admitted.

I said to him, "And you feel His love and are aware of His presence, and that's wonderful. I feel nothing. I feel dead inside. Then there's the depression that comes and goes. I have to take drugs to sleep. Things used to work in my life. Not everything, but I had a life, you know. With enough effort and prayer, stuff was accomplished. Nothing works now. I hate to complain. God has blessed me a bunch. Maybe I'm just spoiled. Maybe I miss my former life, my children, relationships too much. Is that bad? You know that there are plenty of people who would trade with me any day. I guess I had it too good."

"Regardless of your situation, I think you should still have His presence."

"I would love to, but I don't, and I can't lie about it or fake it. I know the difference. I don't have it. I just don't know why."

"Why don't you ask Him?"

"What?"

"Ask *Him* what the problem is."

"*You* ask Him. He talks to you all of the time."

"No, *you* ask Him. I'm sure He wants to speak to you. Why wouldn't He?"

"Fine, Dennis. I'll do this for you. Maybe because *you're* here, He'll answer."

I was getting exasperated. Dennis and I had hoed this row dozens of times, with little to show. I gradually began to feel like I was just humoring him.

So I assumed a perfect sitting prayer position. I was sure that nothing would happen, and I really wanted to prove to Dennis that God would not speak to me. I was intending to impress Dennis with my perfect prayer, and God's total lack of response.

I folded my hands, bowed my head and said, most reverently, "Dear Lord, is there something wrong with my relationship with you? In Jesus' name, amen."

"*There is nothing wrong with our relationship*," came instantly, clearly into my mind. My eyes opened very wide, and Dennis could tell that something was up. He sat straight up. His eyes were as big as saucers.

"Well?" he practically demanded. "Well?"

"I think He spoke to me. I really do," I said, clearly dumbfounded.

"Well? Come on! What did He say?" Dennis was almost levitating off his chair.

"He said quite clearly to me, 'There is nothing wrong with our relationship.'"

"That's it?"

"That's it."

"You're sure He spoke?"

"Dennis, I know His voice. That was God. Absolutely. I'm very surprised. I don't think that He has answered me like that for many years, maybe never. I can't remember a time."

"Wow! So why can't you feel his love? What about that? What's the problem there?"

"I'll ask Him."

"Yeah. Do it," Dennis practically demanded.

"Lord, why can't I feel your love?"

"*You will feel My love when you express My love.*"

I stared straight ahead at the far wall. "You will feel My love when you express My love," I said quietly.

"Wow! That's heavy. Interesting. Hmmm," Dennis responded.

"That wasn't me, Dennis. I don't come up with stuff like that. That was God. I'll have to think about that."

"So you will *feel His love when you express His love.*"

"That's what He said."

"That *is* something to think about. I like it. That makes a lot of sense generally, you know? A little lesson there."

"Yeah, see? That's the kind of stuff I get. Concepts to think about."

"Yeah, I agree. But what about the depression and the failures and the problems you've had with people misunderstanding you? What's the gray cloud all about?"

"Well, I'll ask Him."

"Good deal. You're really on a roll here. Get all you can."

"Lord, why do I feel depressed and have little success and other stuff? In Jesus' name, amen."

"*That's the Devourer and the Maligner,*" came the immediate reply.

"Well? Well?" Dennis could hardly stand any delay in my response.

"Weird."

"What? What? What's weird?"

"He said, 'That's the Devourer and the Maligner.'"

"Who? Devourer? Yeah. But what's the Maligner? What's that?"

"Dennis, this definitely is not me. I don't even recall ever hearing about a Maligner," I said with a frown, as my brain scanned for relevant information.

"What would that be?" he asked again.

"Well, to malign someone is to attempt to bring vicious ill will to them by speaking badly about them, to try to cause them distress or to fail."

"That is definitely something to think about. I've never heard of a Maligner," Dennis said.

"That's what I heard Him say, 'the Devourer and the Maligner.' Interesting though. It sounds like the Enemy's tactics."

"So what should you do?"

"Ask Him?"

"Go for it."

"Lord, what should I do about this Devourer and Maligner?"

"*Rebuke them*," the words came again.

"Well?"

"Rebuke them."

"That's it?"

"Yep."

"Makes sense."

"I guess I'll assume that there is nothing wrong with my relationship with Him, that I will feel His love when I express His love, and I'll rebuke the Devourer and the Maligner. Yeah, that's a lot. I'm gonna be okay, Dennis. Now I have even more to think about."

"You want to pray about all of this?"

"Yeah, let's close this up with some prayer."

9

Portland

Live for the moment, I'm told. That's the way to get through.
Are you kidding? Tell that to someone who is nailed to a cross.

SOMETIME LATE IN the summer of 2005, I became restless. Business was not good, and I no longer sensed a purpose in Coeur d'Alene. Though we had made some progress when I first arrived, our plans to offer increased services through my capabilities were not working. The result was tension between my business partner and me. I decided to look elsewhere for work, mainly on the East Coast.

The West Coast was a possibility, but it was unfamiliar. I had family in the East with whom I could stay while I looked for a job or business. I prayed and set October 1 as when I would place my house on the market and head for Baltimore. It was decision time once more. I was confronted by well-intentioned friends.

"Do you know that God wants you to move back East?" someone asked.

"No," I replied.

"What do you think He wants you to do?"

"He gave me a brain and expects me to use it. I need to work."

"But what does *He* want you to do? Have you prayed and determined His will?"

"He wants me to trust Him and do what I believe I need to do."

"But how are you sure that's what *He* wants? You're making your own decisions."

The question is commonly presented as if God's *will* can be reduced to a succession of events. I don't deny that God's will often includes a succession of events, but those events can take place under different circumstances, and the same event can be triggered by different motivations. The same money can be given, though one gives to impress others, while another gives to please God. Same money, same event, but different motivation.

To do someone's will is to do their pleasure. To do God's will is to do what pleases Him. I don't believe that just following a succession of events is necessarily what God finds pleasing. Assuming that a mere event succession is what God wants results in a certain amount of attempting to read His mind.

"I believe that the Lord wants me to trust Him and make a decision. That's what I'm doing," I answered.

"But what if He wants you to stay here?"

"Why would He? There is no work here. There's no reason to stay here. I have no attachments, no purpose, nothing. This is what I've always done. In lieu of other direction from Him, I know what to do."

It seemed impossible that it could actually be that simple, but it was. It was assumed that I had to get an okay from God to make a significant move. It was not necessary, I'd answered. I'd certainly prayed for wisdom, for Him to intervene if I was making a wrong move, and I'd asked Him to open the right doors. However, I was leaving. I had some money, but not enough to retire on. I needed a job or a business to invest in. It was simple. No divine intervention was necessary.

Wrong again. Divine intervention is what apparently happened.

ON SEPTEMBER 29, two days before I planned to leave, we received a call from a major machine tool manufacturer offering us an expansion of our dealership into Washington and Oregon. Major dealerships were not easy to come by, and it was a valuable offer. Since my business partner was personally well established in Idaho, Montana, and Wyoming, I was the obvious choice to head west and pitch the line to the hundreds of potential customers in the big cities of Seattle and Portland. The timing was a whole day early, but it still looked like God to me.

I did not want to move to the Northwest Coast. Though I loved living in Coeur d'Alene, winters were difficult. Add Christmas, mine and my daughters' birthdays—right after the holidays—to eight months of overcast skies, and it was a depressing mix. Seattle and Portland are famous for rain. I already had gray clouds in my soul and above me for most of the winters in Coeur d'Alene. I feared darker gray clouds filled with rain.

GROWN MEN ARE not supposed to be fearful. We are supposed to be the protectors of our families, warriors, strong and valiant. I was no longer any of those. The fabric of my life had been torn to shreds. I felt as if I were standing on a wobbly platform, and every bump or jostle made me tense and defensive. Though I once had a personal kingdom I ruled over, I now pictured myself like a little, old, homeless man trying desperately to defend what was left in his shopping cart. Irrational? Of course.

Nearly two years earlier, as I was leaving Sheridan, a guy who worked for the company there said some extremely insulting things to me. "You're a real screw-up. You can't do anything right," he said. His opinions should have been meaningless to me. He was a hired hand who had no reliable knowledge about me or my background. At the time, I was shocked. I hung my head and walked away.

I've used my fists more than a few times to make a point. That was before I became a Christian, of course. Now I only think about it occasionally. At those times it would be easier to be small and weak. If I were small and weak, my only option would be to walk away or get myself injured—or worse. Options are a good thing normally, but options can get you into trouble. Money, intelligence, influence, and physical size are strengths of the flesh which we can use to get our own way, to control events, which usually involves persuading others to see things our way. Though these physical assets can be used for God's purposes, they usually serve only our own. Using these assets correctly, which is good stewardship, is a whole lot trickier than we are sometimes led to believe.

So I just hung my head and walked away? Though I would like to believe that I did that out of my love for Jesus, and that I was turning the other cheek, that would not be entirely true. No. It was at least partly because I was beginning to think that perhaps he was right. Try depression sometime. Depression can be *worse* than a nightmare. I never imagined such pain.

NOW, SINCE I could not quite bring myself to actually move to the West Coast, I decided to operate temporarily out of Coeur d'Alene. Over the following six months, through telephone calls and weekly trips to Seattle or Portland, I reduced about four hundred and fifty possible customers to a viable two-fifty or so. Fortunately, I had a friend in Vancouver, Washington, who had a spare room, which saved a bunch on motels. Though I battled wind and rain driving the streets of Seattle and Portland during the bleak, dark winter of 2005–2006, I did not sell a single machine. Certainly one hundred thousand dollar machining and turning centers are not an impulse buy, but not making a single sale was extraordinary.

Though accepting challenges has caused me occasional loss, I have managed to pull off a few things that surprised even me. I don't like hearing *you can't do that*, or *you can't make that work*. Halfway is no way, and I reasoned that I was only going halfway by not opening a local office. I figured we had a responsibility to give the company we represented a better presence. So I researched and found the perfect location in Portland; and, fortified with assurances from our regional manager that the company was behind me 100 percent, I negotiated an eighteen-month lease on a nice office-warehouse combination. I placed my Coeur d'Alene house on the market and bunked in the room rented from my friend. I felt sure that something would come together on the West Coast.

Unknown to me, at nearly the same time, a distributorship was also being given to an additional dealer with lots of dedicated customers. Less than two months after signing the lease, purchasing furniture and setting up shop, I was embarrassed to learn of my competitor as I visited a prospect. I knew the other dealer. Good people. We had lunch and decided there was no way to work together. I'm not stupid. I know when I'm beat, so I closed up. Now my job was to find a job or a business and continue to pay rent for an office for which I had no use. Eighteen months times thirteen hundred dollars a month? More loss.

"Don't freak out. Keep it together," I said to myself, as anxiety rose up to attack. "Keep it together. Breathe."

DURING THAT 2006 summer, a dialogue occurred during a small group discussion at a church in Vancouver, Washington, across the Columbia

River from Portland. A woman was describing her business failure.

"I did everything I could to make sure I was making the right decision. I prayed and asked people to pray for me. I felt and I really believed that it was going to work. But somehow I missed the Lord," she said.

"Why?" I asked.

"Why, what?"

"Why do you think that you missed the Lord?"

"Well, it didn't work. I lost the business, and it was a financial disaster."

"Why is that missing the Lord?"

"Well, it would have worked out. We would have been successful."

"That has nothing to do with it. God does not guarantee success. You can follow the Lord perfectly and fail miserably in many ways."

"I don't understand," she said.

"Who said that God guarantees success? Where does it say that if you pray, you will be successful?"

This is where the actual conversation ended. The following is first composite, and then hypothetical:

"It says so in Matthew 21:22, 'And all things you ask in prayer, believing, you shall receive.'"

"Do you really think that you can ask God for anything, and He will grant you that thing? Does that really make any sense?" I asked.

"Well, not just anything."

"So He will give you some things, but not others?"

"Yes."

"Who decides what He will give and what He won't give?"

"Well, whatever is in His will. We should pray according to His will. If we pray according to His will, He will grant what we ask."

"What is God's will? How do we determine what His will is?" I asked.

"We pray, study His word, and seek counsel."

"So you decided through prayer, or some interpretation of scripture, that it was His will that this particular business be a success?"

"Yes. I believe that He wants us to succeed in the things we do.

I don't know if He said that my business would succeed. I just assumed, I guess."

"Interesting assumption. Is success always a good thing? Would we really ever grow up into mature people if we succeeded at everything we did? Does God really want a bunch of spoiled brats? Isn't it reasonable that He would want us to learn to handle failure, disappointment and frustration?"

"Why? He wants us to prosper," someone else joined in.

"What? Why do we, as contemporary Christians, persist in the erroneous assumption that God's will for our lives is that we be successful, make a bunch of money, have wonderful children who are serving the Lord, have a successful ministry, be out of debt and live securely in a fallen and darkened world? Where did we ever get the idea that He would be pleased to isolate us from all of the pain that the so-called heathen have to suffer? How did Jesus, who declared that we must deny ourselves and take up our cross daily, ever become the One who would make everything work out for us?" I asked.

"We learned most of that from the big-name ministries that arose out of the knowledge revelations in the seventies and eighties, who still teach us to worship faith and knowledge, and to send them our money," the new person said.

"Oh?"

"Is there a problem with that?" he asked.

"Yes, I have lots of problems with that," I said.

"Really? Well, perhaps there is your answer."

"What do you mean? Answer to what?" I asked.

"The answer to what has happened in your life, the business failures, divorce, everything. You believe that God wants you to fail so you can learn some lesson or something. Your lack of faith and belief that God wants the best for you is the problem. You need sound basic teaching. You have the wrong concept of God."

"I do? Who are you?"

"Never mind. You also prayed to trade your present reward for an eternal reward. You're receiving what you prayed for. What's the problem? Quit your complaining. Most people want nice things and a comfortable life. Where did you ever come up with the idea that God wants us to be miserable?"

"I don't believe God wants us miserable."

"That's what *I* heard you saying."

"Oh, really? I said that I *felt* like that sometimes. You know what? Now I know *you*. How did *you* get in here?"

"I come here all the time. Everybody is welcome here."

"Right. You and I have nothing to discuss."

"Why? You'd be surprised. I can make things work, you know."

"No, thanks. Hey, guys, I have to do some grocery shopping before I go back to my room. I'm out of here. As for *you*, get lost."

"Bye—for now."

I TRAVELED BETWEEN Coeur d'Alene and Vancouver often. Though the miles piled up on my pickup, my stuff was still in my house. I needed to touch it once in a while, and I tried to meet with a small group a ways from Coeur d'Alene as often as I could.

"Hi, friends. How are you all this evening?"

"Oh, wonderful. Wonderful. The Lord is certainly good. I'm glad that you could join us. We were just about to go to prayer. Is there anything in particular that we need to pray about for you?"

"I will probably think of some things while you are praying, but go ahead. I can join in when it's appropriate," I said.

"Lord Jesus, thank you for … and we lift up Julia's lovely daughter. Please, bring her to you and help her handle her loss and her anger … and we bring all these needs to you, thanking you for hearing us, believing that you will answer each and every request. In Jesus' name, amen."

"Amen."

"So is anything new, Jonathan? It's been a few weeks. So nice of you to drive all the way here for our little meeting."

"I appreciate your invitation. It's nice to be here. You are a blessing to me."

"We pray often for you."

"Thank you so much. I appreciate your prayers. Uh, Julia?"

"Yes?"

"May I ask a personal question?"

"Sure. What's the question?"

"Would you mind telling me about your daughter? What is she angry about? Forgive me for not remembering, if you have told me before. What happened?"

"Her husband died and left her with their two small children."

"I'm so sorry. Recently?"

"It's been nearly two years."

"That's still pretty recent. How is she coping?"

"Good in some ways. Not so good in others. She's very angry at God, and that worries me."

"Is she a Christian?"

"No, not really. I doubt it."

"But she's angry at God?"

"Yes. She blames Him for her husband's death."

"Why?"

"She wants to blame somebody, so she blames Him, I guess. She believes that He could have prevented it."

"Sure, He could have. Has she talked to Him about it?"

"What do you mean?"

"Has she talked to Him? She's angry at Him. Has she expressed her anger to Him?"

"I don't think so. She doesn't pray."

"If I were her, I would go tell it all to Him. Tell Him exactly what she thinks of His way of handling her life, her husband's death, the whole thing. Let Him have it all."

"You're not serious."

"I am completely serious. It makes no sense to be so angry at someone and not tell them. I wouldn't want someone to be upset with me and not at least present their case. Wouldn't you rather hear it directly?"

"I guess so. Yes, I would rather they come to me if they were upset about something, especially if they blamed me for it. But she's not a Christian."

"So what? It might help her. Surely can't hurt. People should bring their complaints to God. Open up a dialogue. Anything. Talk to Him. Why ignore Him? If she doesn't believe in Him, she should tell Him. That may sound pointless, but suggest to her that she go out and yell at Him, if necessary. He's heard it all anyway."

"Have you done that?"

"Many times. If I told you about the despicable ways that I've addressed God, you might be surprised. It's only by His incredible grace that I'm not a charred lump of burned flesh and bone lying at the top of one of the many hills I've climbed to discuss things with him. I'm not saying it's right. I'm just saying I've been so angry that I couldn't help but tell Him. Have it out with Him. You never know what God might do."

"Maybe I'll suggest it to her."

"I would."

I forgot about the conversation, but in the next week or two I made it to the little gathering again for some encouragement and prayer. After we prayed, Julia said that she had something amazing to report.

"What is it?" I said.

"My daughter. I told her what you said."

"Yes?"

"She wasn't interested at first, but I told her it might do her some good. We talked quite a bit. A few days later she came to me and said, 'I think God spoke to me!'"

"Really?"

"Yes."

"Please, go on."

"Well, she said it seemed ridiculous at first, but I guess she started in on Him and pretty quickly she was really yelling at Him; asked Him why her husband was taken from her when she is so young."

"Wow. What did He say?"

"'So that you and your family could be saved.' Those were the words she said He used."

"Really?"

"Yes. She was stunned. She said she just knew that it was God."

"That's wonderful. Really wonderful. Anything else?"

"No. We haven't talked much about it. I think she wants to think about it."

"Wonderful. I believe that it was God. No doubt about it."

"Yes, she would never say anything like that."

"You know, it never hurts to bring anything and everything to God. Let Him sort through all of it. You never know what He might come up with."

"We'll keep her in our prayers."

"Yeah. I'd like to hear more about what happens."

I have lost touch with this little group since I left the Northwest, but I will get together with them again.

TED, ANOTHER FRIEND, came to Coeur d'Alene during that summer of 2006 for a business meeting of some kind and stayed at my house. I enjoyed talking with Ted. We could talk freely about a lot of things without necessarily having to be nice, though we could do that too. We could banter a bit.

I enjoy good banter among guys. I liked the guys in my previous job shop, and during the twelve years I was an owner, we got sufficiently comfortable with each other to enjoy some ribbing. Some version of the following conversation was not uncommon as I'd enter the welding area:

"Better start looking like you're accomplishing something, boys. The boss is headed this way," the foreman might yell, so I could hear.

"Nice to see that you got these frames welded already. Must have been working," I might say.

"We usually try to get something done around here to keep you office people happy."

"So, what do you really do when we're not around?"

"Drink beer."

"Too bad."

"Why?"

"'Cuz we drink good whiskey in the offices."

"Yeah, but *you're* buying *our* beer."

It was fun, though it took years for acceptance to be won. Small-town pride is encouraged among the Idaho locals, and the local rivalry which makes high school football games highly exciting can carry over into the workplace. Though I was still viewed as an outsider, that the guys would mess with me a little, and that I could retaliate, was a victory for me. Everybody knew I was a Christian, but I wanted to show that my Christianity was more than a mere moral stance. I tried to care for our employees personally, regard them as equals and, within reason, address their humor as not being beneath me. Being able to lighten up is good for us.

Ted and I sat around my house that evening.

"I thought you were being rude," I said.

"What? Rude? When?" he asked.

"The time when we had breakfast with Mary. You sat there and read the paper."

"I wasn't being rude. I was just reading while you were talking to Mary. I thought you two wanted some time to talk."

"Wanted some time to talk? We invited you out to have breakfast. You ignored us and read the newspaper. That's rude."

"Are you going to be nice this evening? I thought it was now your turn to be nice. Is there something on your mind? Why aren't you being nice?"

"You just asked me three questions and made an accusation. Is it nice to start a conversation with an accusation?" I kidded.

"We're not starting. We're already conversing. Besides, you started with an accusation of rudeness."

"You're right. You win," I said smugly.

"Great. I feel much better. So … do you really think that was rude? I didn't mean to be rude. You're rude at times."

"I know. You've let me know that," I admitted, because he was correct. "Now, though, let's talk about you."

"You're leading up to something else. I can tell. What's next? What are you really wanting to talk to me about?"

"Your wife is unhappy."

"She's fine."

"She's unhappy."

"Look, she's fine. You don't know her like I know her. We've been married a long time. She's happy. She just shows it in different ways. I've asked her. She says she's happy. She has lots of stuff to do, and sometimes she gets overloaded. She can be moody, but she's happy. I know it."

"Okay."

Ted thought for a minute and said, "Okay. So why do you think she's unhappy?"

"I just see it. She appears unhappy."

"Why would she be unhappy?"

"I don't really know. I could speculate, but there isn't much point in that. I'm just making an observation about her unhappiness. That's all. I wish someone had come to me and told me that it was so obvious that my wife was unhappy."

"No one did?"

"Not that I can remember. Some said that I wouldn't have listened anyway, but that's a cop-out. Responsible people say things. It's a risk, but I'm seeing, more and more, that it's the right thing to do. So I'm saying something. You can choose to listen or not."

"Would you have listened?"

"Don't know. Maybe. Maybe—if someone I trusted spoke to me. But that's another story for another time. This is now. How about you?"

"I think you're wrong. I think that you see what you want to see, and that you have a lot of pain, and that you perceive things wrongly through that pain."

"Okay."

"Do you agree?"

"No. Look. I'm making an observation based on what I see. Do what you want. Convincing me that I'm wrong, if you could—and you can't—will not change anything. There is usually some truth in people's observations. They may be magnified or distorted by their own issues, but sincere people don't risk conflict for no reason. I'm your friend. I like you. I appreciate your friendship, but, in my observation, your wife is unhappy.

"You know, the Jews and the church have a long history of executing messengers. We still do it. Discredit or kill the messenger, as if that will get rid of the problem. I love it. The messenger is the *real* problem. Doggone prophets! Can't we find some decent ones around here who will tell us pleasant things, words we want to hear? What's with them anyway? Can't they mind their own business? What arrogance! Do they think they're sent from *God* or something?" I said, only partly joking.

"Okay, okay. I'll talk to her."

"What? And try to convince her that she's happy? Ted, my friend, you may convince *yourself* that she's happy, but she will still be unhappy."

"What do you suggest?"

"Love her."

"I do. I tell her a lot."

"For you, or for her?"

"How should I love her?"

"That's your project."

"I'll ask her how she wants to be loved."

"Wrong."

"Come on, Jonathan, I'm kidding. You know I'm kidding."

"I hope so."

We sat in silence for a few minutes. "Sometimes I think women want us to read their minds," Ted mused audibly.

"They do. They kind of expect us to. Women have told me that."

"We can't."

"I think they are really asking us to take the time and interest to learn what they really want. Maybe even venture into some uncharted emotional waters."

"Sounds risky."

"Why?"

"Women remember everything. Make a mistake and you're doomed to hear about it for the rest of your life."

"That's a whole other deal, Frank. Be dangerous. Women like dangerous men. We should all be more dangerous, especially as Christians."

"You think women like dangerous men?"

"In some ways. I'm not talking about *physically* dangerous, like scary or something. I mean *living* somewhat dangerously, like taking some risks emotionally. I think there is a longing in most of us to live more on the edge, though maybe I'm wrong. It's just a thought. Some of us have the opportunity, personality, arrogance or stupidity to actually do it. But yes, I believe women see men who live a little dangerously as manly, romantic, unpredictable."

"Maybe, but not all women."

"I'm not sure. Perhaps we'll talk about this more later. It will be interesting," I said.

"Why is unpredictable better?"

"We like routine and predictability, but adventure implies chance and the possibility of loss of control, newness. That's dangerous."

"But that's a privilege few have access to. Most of us are just trying to keep our lives in order."

"But there you go. *We* are keeping our lives in order. Where does God fit in? God is *always* there. So you make a mistake. So you tried. You know, the best stories are told about things that didn't go right."

"Yeah. We boast about our successes, but the most fun is in finding humor in those brushes with death, though it's always way after the actual incident. So you think we should be more dangerous as Christians?"

"I'm not sure that *dangerous* is the correct word, maybe more risky, but we should certainly be more salty. Jesus said that."

"Salt does change the flavor of food. We should be changing the flavor of the world with our Christianity."

"Yet it seems as if the world has done more flavoring of modern Christianity."

"But Christian principles originally flavored the formation of this nation."

"Yeah, but I'm not talking about Christian principles. Those can end up being laws. Christian principles can be used for all kinds of purposes," I said.

"You know, actually, God *is* dangerous. Yeah, the churches like to present Him as pretty user-friendly, but He is very dangerous. I seldom hear that message come across," Ted said.

"A user-friendly God. Hmm. That's good. Can I use that?"

"Sure, use it anywhere you want. I'm going to bed. See you in the morning."

"What about your wife?"

"I heard you, and thanks."

"Thanks for listening."

Ted went for a quick run the next morning, and we went out together for some breakfast.

"How's your breakfast, Ted?"

"Good. How's yours?"

"Good. I like IHOP."

"Yeah, I don't need the pancakes, but they're sure good. This is a nice place. I like IHOP too. Hey, Jonathan, the Lord gave me some words for you this morning while I was out."

"Really? He gave you some words?"

"Yep. Would you pass the strawberry syrup? I like that strawberry syrup on these buttermilk pancakes."

"The Lord gave you a word?" I said, passing the syrup.

"Words. Yeah, three things. Are you going to eat your toast? Looks pretty good. Want your toast?"

"Stay away from my toast. What did He say? What?"

"The Lord?"

"Come on, Ted. What?"

"Oh, He only said that He was pleased with you, that there was nothing wrong with your relationship with Him, and that you were making up for lost time."

"Really?"

"Real as rain."

"That's all He said?"

"That's it. Could you signal that waitress over there? Hey, 'scuse me. I need some water. Do you want your water?"

"Drink my water. What could that mean? What could He mean by that?"

"What?"

"Making up for lost time."

"I have no idea."

"None?"

"Nothing. That's just exactly what He said. That's all I know."

"Well, you could have thought up the first two. We may have discussed that. I've already heard some things like that. But the last is new. Definitely. I know you wouldn't just come up with that, but I have no idea what 'making up for lost time' refers to."

"You're right, and I haven't a clue what He's implying either. Honestly. Makes no sense to me. Pray about it. Maybe He'll fill you in."

"I believe you. I'll ask Him."

"Great. Hey, I have to hit the road. Thanks for the bunk and the company. Give me a call if you get anything on the *lost time* thing."

"Well, thanks for coming; and you bet, I'll let you know."

What could *that* mean? I prayed, "Lord, what did you mean by *making up for lost time?*"

I went back to my house to mow the lawn. I had lived in Coeur d'Alene, Idaho for over three years by then, since the spring of 2003. I liked Coeur d'Alene. Though it was gradually becoming more of a tourist town, it was absolutely preferable to living on the East Coast. I thought about the time when I arrived and remembered wondering which house to buy. I wanted to own a house, at least for an investment, so I prayed after looking at five or six possibilities within my price range. I had no idea what to buy. I had always left that up to my wife. I really didn't care that much. It had been important to her, but not really to me. How was I supposed to make a decision? I had no criteria.

WHEN I FIRST arrived in Coeur d'Alene, I had a few rooms full of furniture from the Denver townhouse, and I had to pick out a suitable house. I did not want to pay rent when I could afford to buy. But what did I need? I didn't cook. I tried that. Cooking was not worth the effort. I enjoy good food. I do. Cathie was an excellent cook. She made everything taste good. Well, most things—you know.

But after losing over thirty-five pounds on the divorce diet, when food tasted like warmed topsoil, and my clothes hung on my diminished frame, a friend finally remarked, "Hate to tell you, brother, but the gaunt look is not in." I forced myself to eat good food that tasted terrible. Why waste good food, I thought? So I ate canned soup, and as my appetite eventually recovered, I moved up to frozen entrees. They aren't bad—honestly.

So what were the criteria for buying a house? I preferred some distance from my neighbors but not a lot of lawn to mow. A large garage might be nice, but it could be a dangerous collection area. A fireplace would be nice, if I had somebody to enjoy it with. Patio, deck, swimming pool? I really didn't care. I just needed a place to live. Leaning toward a good investment didn't help. I knew little about real estate investing.

I stopped by the side of the road to pray. Though I was not accustomed to getting direct answers from God, I barely clasped my hands to pray when one of the houses I was considering appeared to me almost visually. It was remarkable. I assumed that God had spoken, and I bought the house. I had no idea how significant the house would be. A year later, when we had to move our business into the house for a few months, it was perfect. We then rented office space within a half mile from that house. For many other reasons it was obvious that God knew exactly which house was necessary, and He had let me know.

It was easy to see His guiding hand, looking back at what had passed. I could not see those confirming signs, but they were all there. It was as if they were facing the wrong way, as if they could only be read from one direction—looking back. Must be the *hindsight* thing. Yes, I was sure that, in His unseen way, God had been guiding every move.

I was right where He wanted me to be. At least I was sure of that.

NOW, I WAS mowing the lawn for possibly one of the last times. My life in Coeur d'Alene was definitely drawing to a close. I mowed the front and made about four or five laps around the back when He came online.

"All that time that you were running a business, putting your children through college, leading Bible studies, being successful?"
"Uh, yes?"
"Sandbox."

I'm not sure exactly where the sandbox came in. It seems like it should have been then, but I could have seen the sandbox earlier. Now the real significance became apparent.

"Sandbox?!"
"Mostly wasted. Now you're making up for lost time."

I was stunned! Wasted? Sandbox? Not even elementary school? What could this mean? Sandbox? He was certainly implying that I was out of the sandbox now, but I had no idea how far out. Was I just hanging over the edge? The last nearly five years, this *making up for lost time* was nothing but pain and failure. Nothing worked.

Sure! Now it all fit. I always have it backwards. He told me that. It's there again. Failure is success. The kingdom of God. Personal reduction in process. Trial by fire. All in the Bible.

I told Ted about what God had said to me. He considered it to be a fit with the other things we thought the Lord was saying. Yes, God was addressing maturity. Ted and I were talking again, another time.

He said, "You enjoy thinking, don't you?"
"Yeah, I guess. Doesn't everybody?" I replied.
"No. Not like you. You use your mind like a playground. You think for recreation."
"Are you some kind of mind reader?"

"You know I am a psychologist."

"Hmm. I used to enjoy thinking, but I don't know what to think about anymore. How can I think if I don't know what the game is or what the rules are?"

"Interesting … He even took away your playground."

"Interesting to you, maybe."

If I had been at only *sandbox* level all those years, if that was all wasted time, what could possibly lie ahead? I couldn't envision any kind of future I wanted to look at.

I WAS ANGRY. I had been angry. I may have deserved divorce and maybe it was time to move on in business. But wasn't it time for something to work out? I wanted to find the Lord in all of this, but I was wavering. Joan is another composite friend.

"Hey, Joan."

"Hi, Jonathan"

"Joan, do you ever get angry at God?"

"No. Never. Why would you ask that?"

"Just wondering."

"God is good. He loves us and would never do anything to make us angry at Him. Jesus died for us. How could anyone be angry at someone who sacrificed so much for us? That's just not right. I love Him so much. He means everything to me. I would never have a reason to be angry at Him."

"Okay. Okay. I believe you."

"Are you angry at God, Jonathan?"

"Yes."

"You need to get over that. Why would you be angry at God? What has He done that you should be angry?"

"Destroyed my life."

"Destroyed your life? Come on. Do you blame God for what's happened to you? Do you think that your nightmare was His doing?"

"Absolutely."

"You're wrong. God doesn't cause businesses to fail and break up relationships. That's you, and you just want to blame it on Him. That's all it is."

"Okay. So God is all about doing good things?"

"Right. He wants to bless us. He wants us to have a good life."

"What about Job?"

"What about him?"

"His life was wrecked."

"That was his self-righteousness. You know that. Job feared losing, and he got what he feared. We shouldn't live in fear. Job brought his own calamity upon himself."

"You really believe that?"

"Well, it's true, isn't it?"

"No. Not a bit of it. God described Job's righteous ways to Satan who accused Job of responding only to God's blessings, saying that he would curse God if the blessings were removed. God placed Job in Satan's hands, except for a few limitations."

"Well, God wouldn't have done that without a reason."

"So God might do something harmful if He had sufficient reason?" I asked.

"You're missing the point. God didn't do it. Satan did it. Satan implied that Job only served God because God blessed him. God wanted to show Job's faithfulness."

"To whom?"

"To Satan."

"Why to Satan? That makes no sense to wreck someone's life to prove a point to Satan."

"Well, to the heavens then, or to the world, someone."

"But people have the wrong idea about what happened. I hear too often that it was Job's fault, so what has the world learned if the world has the wrong idea about what happened? Anyway, God gave His permission to Satan, and so He let Satan harm him. Would you let someone harm your child?"

"No, but Job was a grown man."

"So it's okay for a grown man to be harmed by the most powerful being ever created?"

"I'm sure God had His reasons."

"So God gave His permission, making Him responsible. Look,

Job even tried to present his case to God because he knew that God was responsible. Later, God said that Job had spoken correctly of Him."

"You're reaching."

"I don't think so. Joan, if stuff goes on that is out of God's control, we're in big trouble. Think about it. If the devil and his minions are free to do their will, then they would do away with anyone who resisted them. We wouldn't stand a chance. God controls everything."

"But that's why we have to pray for one another, for protection. We pray hedges around our children, our finances, our homes and churches. We pray for God's angels to protect us from evil. Why do we pray about those things?"

"That's an excellent question. Do you suppose that Job forgot to pray?"

"I think he did pray, but there was a problem, and maybe his prayers weren't heard. He feared, and we shouldn't pray in fear. We should believe, and God will hear our prayers and act. Job must have doubted, because he feared."

"So just because we have fear, our prayers won't be answered? Do you realize how dumb this stuff sounds? What kind of God would hold us to such standards? Back in the eighties when I was struggling financially, I actually had someone tell me that I had tied God's hands! Can you see it? Little me, tying the hands of the One who spoke the universe into existence! That's the height of absurdity."

"Okay, that does sound somewhat stupid," she admitted.

"It is. Now we have people who feel left out, like they fell off the Christian blessing train. I've heard from them. Sure, many may have caused their own problems, but many are suffering trials and tribulations that far exceed any cause-and-effect scenario. Many are actually being tried by God. They feel bewildered and rejected, like they don't measure up in some way. I have to believe that God is bigger than our understanding. He wouldn't exclude someone because they are fearful, unable to comprehend some complex spiritual principle, or are unable to meet some fake standard."

"But there are spiritual principles. There are some standards."

"Yes, and I'm not arguing that. Can we just look at the story of Job? I'm concerned about one issue for now, and Job is the best example, though the story of Joseph is similar."

"Okay, how do you see Job?"

"I've read some books. They didn't mean much until I found myself in my present situation. I wish I could remember everything I read. But I do remember reading a lot that God is a good God. He blesses people. He does only good things. Satan does all the evil things. That seems pretty juvenile to me. Satan does nothing without God's permission. I see Job as an honest man who loved God, and God wanted to bless him."

"Okay."

"So He tried him."

"What do you mean?"

"God tried him, put him through a trial."

"How?"

"By allowing the devil to destroy nearly everything."

"How is that blessing Job? Job was already blessed."

"Yes, in a way. Listen. First, God demonstrated to Job, and to the devil, I guess, whatever, that Job's obedience was unconditional, not based on what God did for him. God did that purposely. He knew exactly what He was doing. God always knows exactly what He is doing, and nothing happens to us without God's knowing it and being okay with it."

"But Job was angry with God."

"Yes, I believe that he was, though I don't see it as directly indicated. He admitted bitterness."

"That was wrong."

"I don't know. All I know is that, at the end of the book, God said that Job's accusers had not spoken correctly of Him as Job had. So apparently God approved of what Job said."

"You're implying that it is all right to complain to God."

"I am. Definitely."

"He wasn't too happy about the Israelites' grumbling. What about that?"

"Maybe I am reaching here, but grumbling is different. If you have a complaint, be open and take it directly to the responsible person. Don't merely complain about your situation."

"And you believe God is responsible, so you complain to Him."

"Yes. Joan, my behavior has not been exemplary. It's been despicable too often. I've said things no man has any business saying to God. God has every right to reject me. Period. He does. I know that. His grace is my only hope. But His grace *is* sufficient for the worst sins. We should *never* feel that there is anything we can't bring to Him."

"But your anger? I think that you have some serious issues you need to work out, or get help with or something. What good does it do to be angry at God? That can't be healthy. I've heard that depression is repressed anger. Maybe that's why you're depressed."

"But my anger is not repressed. I'm telling you about it, and I've expressed it to God."

"Well, then, stop being angry."

"Easy to say; hard to do."

"Jonathan, you can't or shouldn't be angry at God."

"Yeah, I've read that in books."

"And?"

"You know what? I'm sick of some books. Too many books I read seem to end in a formula. Somebody has it rough, and they come up with a solution. They pray a certain way, their circumstances resolve and bingo; time to write a book, complete with the formula on how to solve every related problem. I've talked to lots of people whose situations haven't been resolved. What about them? Are they inferior somehow? Does God dislike them? Are they out of favor with God? More than half of the marriages today end in divorce. Where are all of the happy endings? Sure, many find someone else. I want to also, but a happy ending isn't reality for most of the world.

"Some people are making a lot of money feeding us feel-good formulae for getting God to make our lives work out, and people buy books hoping the formulae will work. Convince people that they need fixing and sell them a solution! I know of very few seriously wounded people for whom the formulae have worked, and I haven't been living in a cave. Too many people are in debt up to their ears, pornography is rampant, divorce is more common than marital success, mega ministries are robbing God and hard-working people of their money by calling it tithing, and you're saying I shouldn't be angry. Jesus made a whip and went after the money changers in the temple. Did He have issues? What's different here?" I asked.

"Jonathan, I'm sorry. There are certainly excesses everywhere, but your anger is at God. You're blaming Him."

"You're right. Okay. I blame God for what happened in my personal life. But I'm also disappointed in churches and their inability to sensitively respond to people who have experienced life-changing trauma. Big difference. I'm not blaming the church. I'm criticizing it. Should we simply ignore indifference or denial because it's related to a church rather than an individual? A church is a bunch of individuals. Are those individuals less accountable simply because they call themselves a church? People criticize my behavior. Is criticizing church behavior a sin?"

"Probably not."

"I'm not on a vendetta, but you wanted to know why I'm angry, and I told you."

"So … how is God being robbed? You said that some ministries were robbing God."

"Do you tithe?"

"Of course."

"Good. You should. What do you suppose that money is used for?"

"To support the work of the ministry."

"Which is?"

"I don't know. Get people saved, teach the word, help people who are in need, I suppose."

"Where do you think the money comes from for the lavish wardrobes and expensive homes owned by the TV preachers?"

"My tithe money goes to my local church."

"Good for you. Listen, Joan, I don't want to be angry, and I'm not really angry about the televangelists. They can do what they want. Perhaps they're getting their reward now, and in full. I'm angry about my personal situation and I see a lot of pain in too many others that's not addressed. So I'm overly sensitive to possible abuses of tithes and offerings. Guilty as charged. But what should I do with my anger? Help me here."

"Lay it down at the cross. We need to take everything to the cross and lay it down there at the feet of Jesus. Give it up to Him."

"I can't find that in the Bible."

"What?"

"Laying stuff down at the cross. We're told to lay stuff aside."

"You're impossible. You pick out every little phrase to find fault with."

"Okay, fine. So I'm also overly sensitive to useless phrases, but do you have any idea how foolish some of this probably sounds to the world?"

"We're all fools for Christ."

"The preaching of the cross is foolishness to the perishing, though I think sometimes it's foolishness to us. Christianity is not foolishness in any way. We're supposed to be full of wisdom and good works, not look like fools. Look, I'm not trying to be a hard case here. God has done many wonderful things in my life. Absolutely wonderful. I believe that He has kept me from harm many times, and that He has watched over me from birth. I believe that He is absolutely holy, pure, right and justified in whatever He does. Absolutely."

"Then why are you still angry?"

"*God destroyed my life*! Weren't you ever angry at your parents?"

"Sure."

"Did you still love them?"

"Yes."

"Are you still angry at them for anything?"

"Maybe for some things, a little."

"Why?"

"They weren't perfect. They made mistakes. Some things really hurt. They were never resolved. But that's my *parents*. That's not *God*."

"So what good is there in being angry at them?"

"None, really. I just feel that way."

"You should forgive your parents. Everybody should forgive their parents. That should be mandatory, like the second part of the sinner's prayer, to forgive our parents. Too many people are still blaming their parents for absurd issues. People should go on a forgiving rampage and hold no person to blame for their circumstances. Take everything, including their anger, to God. He's the One who can do something about it. You know what anger is defined as?"

"What?"

"An emotional state induced by displeasure. Even God gets angry. Anger is not a sin, you know."

"Do I know that? I guess I know that."

"Do you? Then is my anger at God a sin? Am I sinning against God by being angry at Him?"

"Now I'm not sure."

"Look, I'm displeased with the havoc God has allowed what's-his-name to wreak in my life, and He knows it. That's all. He knows I'm not pleased, and I can't hide my displeasure. I'm not certain that God wants me to hide it."

"Why?"

"Think about this … Who is it better to be angry at, God or your parents?"

"Neither. We shouldn't be angry."

"Come on."

"I don't know. It's pretty pointless to remain angry at people. They don't care."

"And they are probably not going to do anything toward resolution. They probably can't. They probably don't care."

"Probably not," she admitted.

"But God *can* do something. God can deal with our anger. If we see Him as guiding our destiny, then we begin to see that people have no ability to hinder our real life. All they can do is cause us discomfort. Sure, they can hurt us, even kill us, but it all has to be in God's plan. Unpleasant experiences are going to come. God assures us that we will have tribulation. God allows what He allows. It's Him. He's in full control. I've heard people say that God is like a landlord and only responds to situations when we ask Him to. That's ridiculous. He's running everything."

"I can't agree. We need to learn how to pray and how to live by His principles."

"Absolutely. We need to be responsible stewards and all that. I'm not addressing that here. I'm addressing maturity."

"Maturity? How?"

"To see God as the good guy and the devil as the bad guy is childish. It's like a good-cop-versus-bad-cop routine. God disciplines us. Face it. And He can use some nasty things to train us. As young children, we don't understand our parents' discipline of us. I don't really understand God's discipline, so I'm angry, perhaps like a child. But I'm not going to make up some fake excuse for God. He doesn't have to meet my standards for me to obey Him."

"So you're angry in the same way you say that Job was angry? What did God do about Job's anger?"

"That's the good part."

"What?"

"God did not address Job's complaints or anger at all. God addressed Job's smallness, his inability to affect much in creation."

"What are you saying?"

"I think it goes together. When God destroys, He builds something better. Yes, He blessed Job twice over in the natural, but Job got the opportunity to see how incomparable God is. Job's understanding, his perception of God was radically altered."

"So Job couldn't see God properly unless He first brought Job to a lower level?"

"Yeah, but remember, the kingdom of God works in reverse. A lower situational level is a higher spiritual level."

"Who wants to hear this?"

"Not me, really. But it's true. It's everywhere in the Bible. It's like God has to delete a bunch of information on our internal hard drive before we can deal with the new information. We get a new operating system when we get saved, but we fill our memory up with knowledge. Like Adam in the garden, we immediately head for the tree of the knowledge of good and evil and download a system of standards. God wants us to be filled with Him, and He is infinite. He goes way beyond knowledge."

"So, your anger?"

"Maybe God's still updating. He said to me directly that He would finish this. He told me that. I just don't know when He will be finished. It feels like it's taking forever."

"Must be a major update."

"Five years?!"

"Slow connection? Maybe you're on dial-up ... Sorry."

"Funny. Yeah. That could be the problem. Hey, Joan?"

"Yeah?"

"Take care."

"Bye."

10

Compromise

They say that close counts in horseshoes and hand grenades.
What about Christianity?

AROUND 1982, WHEN we were living in Grangeville, my wife and I were driving east on US Highway 12. We were on our way to Montana to visit a couple whom the Lord had indicated to me, several years earlier, He would use to teach me some things. I had watched this couple in ministry, as I often led the worship for them at their camp meetings. The Lord frequently displayed His power through their ministry.

I was amused at God's choice of teachers. It was around 1979 that I first ran into them as they exited their baby-blue Cadillac with *King's Kid* on the license plate frame. The man, dressed in a blue leisure suit and shiny black shoes, smiled as he walked past me in my bell-bottoms and sandals. For several years, we made an interesting team, the ex-corporate executive preaching faith and the bearded one playing worship music with a honky-tonk beat. I often complained to the Lord about the prosperity teaching presented at the camp meetings, but He was not interested in my opinion. My orders from Him were to play the piano. So I did, and I was blessed to experience His presence and observe His supernatural gifts in operation often during many meetings.

I played some of the crummiest pianos I'd seen in years at the small churches and rented halls the couple often used. The pianos reminded me of the ones I tore my fingers on while performing with the band around Baltimore in my teen years. Inexpensive, reasonable-sounding portable keyboards were not yet available in the early eighties, and I could not afford what was on the market at the time.

I disliked playing the often out-of-tune monsters with the occasional loose and dangerously sharp keys. I don't read music, so I have to be able to hear some of what I'm playing, and it often sounded awful to me. Several times I remember not wanting to look at the people, who, I feared, must have been wondering what I thought I was doing. However, when I would look up, invariably they would be lost in worshiping the Lord and certainly feeling His presence.

Less of me meant more of Him. In fact, it became quite apparent that the quality of the worship was usually inversely proportional to the quality of the equipment I had. With good equipment and some decent keyboard work, I could get the crowd up dancing. But God seemed to show up more when I struggled to get much of anything from an old upright.

At those times, at least, He preferred simplicity. Now, according to most of the mega-churches I've observed, one would suppose that God prefers lavish multi-media presentations with some of the slickest musicians and best equipment in the business.

Everybody loves a great show. Why wouldn't He?

BUT BACK IN 1982, I felt that there was a problem in my spiritual life, and I was hoping I could get some insight from this same couple. My prayer life seemed to have come to a dead end and my relationship with my Lord was not going well. As we were driving along about twenty miles west of Lolo Pass, God spoke right through the windshield.

"You compromised," He said.

"Me? Compromise? Where did I compromise? What have I done?"

"I placed you in [a particular church] as a standard, and you compromised. I never asked you to become a [conformer to that church]."

I was stunned. I had been admonished by God on a few occasions, but this was a clear rebuke. I immediately knew everything I needed to know about the problems in my spiritual life and the action I needed to take. In addition to the almost audible rebuke, He placed a whole package of information in my brain. We continued on to Montana to counsel and pray with our friends, but I had a course correction to make and I knew my direction. I'll explain what led up to the rebuke in just a bit.

I HAVE LEARNED to regard compromise as a serious issue with implications reaching far beyond the immediate error. Having discovered earlier that my sin was a problem to me and not to God, I once prayed that He would teach me the depth of my sin. Why I asked such a thing, I do not know, but I felt that there were consequences that went beyond the issues of mere morality and integrity.

I began to see merely avoiding sin as like constantly removing the fruit from a bad tree. As the tree matures, the process becomes more laborious, more difficult to hide so much bad fruit. The stuff is everywhere. Some can be hidden among the branches and some can be renamed or covered over with "good works." Of course, the tree is the problem. Christianity 101. But there is another, a less obvious problem—being on the wrong road.

A few years ago I read *The Ezekiel Option*, by Joel Rosenberg, in which a statement by a Jewish rabbi grabbed my attention. He commented about our being able to have our desire or our destiny. I contemplated desire versus destiny for quite some time and felt that it was an important concept. Desire and destiny are both directly and indirectly addressed in the Bible. Desire can refer to our own separate will or pleasure which may conflict with God's will or pleasure. Destiny refers to that which God has planned for us from the beginning, which is offered to us and referred to in Romans, among other places.

> And we know that God causes all things to work together for good to those who love God, to those who are called according to His purpose. For whom He foreknew, He also predestined to become conformed to the image of His Son, that He might be the first-born among many brethren; and whom He predestined, these He also called; and whom He called, these He also justified; and whom He justified, these He also glorified. (Romans 8:28–30)

In the simplest terms I can use, the Biblical narrow road leads to the destiny God has prepared for us. Compromising is one very significant way that we can deviate from that narrow road. The implications are huge, but it is beyond the scope of my purposes here to elaborate much. It is sufficient to emphasize that God's plan, our destiny, the narrow road, is the road of no compromise.

There are trials and there are tests. The tests we encounter determine our position, reveal our tendencies and expose what rules over us. Trials are differentiated from tests in that they create stress and pressure which, if allowed to run their course, produce strength and endurance. Tests can be decision points, road junctions, where making the correct choice means continuing on the narrow road to destiny. If compromise is necessary to continue in the same direction, we must be willing to change direction.

Consider the following verse:

> No temptation has overtaken you but such as is common to man; and God is faithful, who will not allow you to be tempted beyond what you are able, but with the temptation will provide the way of escape also, that you may be able to endure it. (1 Corinthians 10:13)

The *way of escape* can be the new, correct direction. Trials display our mettle, while tests reveal our essence or basic values. When tempted or tested, we are offered choices. Those choices determine our direction, the road we will travel. Often the above scripture is quoted as, "God will not give us more than we can stand." Really? God chastens, defeats, and breaks some by subjecting them to much more than they can stand. Is not *refining* the heating of metal until its constituents separate? Imagine having your constituents separated.

The above scripture also reveals that we always have the ability to choose the right road. The following scripture declares that we are not subject to the laws of action and consequences; rather, we are subject to grace and freedom from bondage:

> For sin shall not be master over you, for you are not under law, but under grace. (Romans 6:14)

Sin, therefore, has no actual mastery over us, no actual power.

This issue of compromise is critical. God may forgive the actual compromise, the sin, but the compromiser may still be on the wrong road. That is a way that sin can be a serious problem to us. Though the sin itself is a problem, being on the wrong road is a *very serious* problem.

I have begun to appreciate how much effort, how many changes might be necessary to get someone back, all the way back, on the right road.

THE COMPROMISE THAT the Lord was rebuking me for came as the result of our attending a conventional church. Sometime in 1982, I became aware that God wanted our family to attend a particular church in Grangeville. Every time I drove past the church, He would draw my attention to it. One day I shared with Cathie that I thought God wanted us to attend the church, which was home to much of Grangeville's upper crust. At that time we definitely lived somewhere down below the pie filling. To the disdain of our more "spiritual" friends, we went to this church. It was a pleasant, refreshing break from the nondenominational, almost ad hoc fellowships we were accustomed to.

I spent many years attending a Methodist church when I was growing up. I was confirmed there and know and love the standard hymns. The choir was absolutely awesome and the huge organ filled the sanctuary with a breath-taking range of frequencies from crystal-clear bells to inaudible lows which could only be felt. Simply reading all of the verses of many hymns sung in traditional churches is proof enough that depth and revelation were abundant hundreds of years ago when the songs were written. I still love to play them. In many ways it was a delight to attend another traditional church. I was excited.

Just a few weeks after our first visit to the new church, I found myself at a meeting in the church basement with a bunch of people that I didn't know. I haven't a clue how I got there, and I remember wondering what I was doing. The people in the group were discussing some meetings scheduled for the coming weekend and they were lamenting that they didn't have any music. Their music team couldn't make it. The leader asked if anyone could play. I didn't say anything, because I didn't really play traditional church music. I mean, I thought they were looking for an organist, or a choir director, or something out of my league.

Well, eventually I raised my hand and told them that I did play the piano. They asked who I was. I told them my name and that I wasn't sure why I was at the meeting, but I said that I played scripture songs. They asked if they were like choruses, which they were. It turned out that they were a group of charismatic church members from out of town who were having a series of revival meetings the coming weekend at that church. They asked if I could play a few songs.

I was delighted to help in the worship for the weekend. It went so well that the pastor asked me to do a song or two during the Sunday services. For a while I had my little spot in the program where I would play guitar and lead the congregation in a chorus or two. I led a little mini-worship, taught the high school kids and generally followed the script.

This went on for several months, during which time I also enjoyed needling the pastor. Doggone it, he was too easy, way too easy. Among other things, he was a stickler for obeying the laws, like the speed limit. One time he was doing at least fifteen mph over the limit to avoid our being late for a Bible study. I asked what the deal was, why he was speeding, and he replied that we were late and he'd promised the leader that he wouldn't be late anymore. So I said that breaking a promise must have been a bigger sin than speeding. He was not amused. I was already on his watch list for, among other things, challenging the students and others at the church to step outside the church boundaries in seeking the Lord.

After he got on my case enough times, I dropped the attitude and decided to toe the line. I quit pointing out what I saw as discrepancies between what he was preaching and what was, to me, sound doctrine, quit trying to teach stuff that he didn't want me to teach the kids and generally went with the flow. In a few weeks, I started noticing that my prayers seemed to be bouncing back off the ceiling and my spiritual life with the Lord was deteriorating. This led to the trip to Montana and the Lord's rebuke.

Then I knew that, at the least, I had to give better answers to the youths I was teaching and to people at the church who asked me questions, answers that I knew would be disagreeable to the pastor. So I repented and asked God for another chance.

A few weeks later, when it was time for me to read a scripture during the Sunday service, the Lord told me to read out of Revelation, specifically one of the letters to the churches. So I decided to read the letter to the church at Laodicea, which accuses the Laodiceans of being lukewarm, probably considered the most critical of the seven letters. The Lord, however, instructed me to read the letter to the church at Ephesus, which accuses the Ephesians of having left their first love. Though I actually turned to the Laodicean letter, wanting to be more critical, He was adamant. It was Ephesus.

So I spoke to the congregation, saying that I believed that what I was about to read was for this church, and read the letter to the church at Ephesus. The pastor was livid. At the end of the service, as we left the building, a lady approached me. She said that it was apparent that I was unaware of the significance of the message in the letter. She was correct. I had no knowledge of that church's history. She said the letter fit that particular church exactly. That very church had apparently once been on fire for God, and she thanked me for the reading. She said that it was definitely a word from the Lord.

GOD USES SPECIFIC words for a reason, I have learned. It has been useful in understanding the implications of His words to me to look up a dictionary definition of the key words and consider the applications. *Compromise*, according to Merriam-Webster, means essentially as follows:

> *1 a*: settlement of differences by arbitration or by consent reached by mutual concessions
>
> *1 b:* something intermediate between or blending qualities of two different things
>
> 2: concession to something derogatory or prejudicial, a compromise of principles

After reading the above definitions a few times, it is not hard to conclude that to be rebuked by the Lord for compromising is not a small matter. There is nothing in any of the definitions which is acceptable to us as Christians. For argument, I will assume I was guilty of all three aspects.

Leaving definition *1a* aside for a moment, consider definition *1b*. I was accused of blending the qualities of two different things. The quality of our Christianity certainly refers to the very essence of our position between the kingdom of God and the kingdom of this world. Quality goes not to appearance or perception, but to the root value of something. I stood accused of blending the root values of two different things. Apparently, there was a difference between my root values and the root values of the church leadership. One could argue, I suppose, that God was saying I had compromised their standard, that *theirs* was the correct standard. To avoid any such confusion, He did add that He had never told me to become a conformer. Definition *2* clearly indicates a concession of principles. Principles are basic. Nothing good there.

Definition *1a* could inspire reasonable debate. Few of us want to be considered as rigid, unteachable, or dogmatic. The very practice of negotiation, so critical for conducting business, is the art of measured compromise. What could be wrong with considering the issues, the desires held by the pastor of the church, and negotiating a solution acceptable to both of us? If the issues had not been related to the quality of my faith, I would have had no problem compromising, I suppose. The problem became one of separating out the values that truly determined the quality of my Christianity. Fortunately, at the time, I did not have to examine the whole spectrum of what was truly essential in my walk with God. When the Lord rebuked me, He added the words *set you as a standard*, which indicated to me that, at least for this particular situation, I was to remain immovable.

How could I be a standard? In what manner was I to remain immovable? It would have been preposterous to expect others to adopt my position on Biblical doctrines, my more contemporary worship style, or my casual dress code. Certainly I was not helping matters by needling the reverend, or displaying a superior spirituality, which I was guilty of. One observant older woman confronted me directly about my attitude. She was spot-on, accusing me of considering myself to be above those who were not hip to the latest choruses and cutting-edge revelations from God. It was true, so I was not a particularly wonderful example of a humble Christian. My *example* was certainly not the standard.

Who was I trying to please? I was apparently not trying to please the physical church authority, or God (according to Him), or my fellow Christians, who disapproved of my church selection. The only one left to please was me.

How was I trying to please me? That particular church was not fulfilling my personal spiritual needs. The preaching was, well, uninteresting. And singing only the first and last verses of those wonderful old hymns? Get real. It was not inspiring. So why was I staying? Then it dawned on me. I had compromised for comfort and complacency. It was good enough, I had decided. God had directed me to that church for a purpose, and I had settled in and made it a place to perform some religious duties—warm a pew.

Pew warming felt preferable to the criticism and disfavor I experienced from the leaders of the independent fellowships we had been attending. At the time, the Grangeville area had been visited by several charismatic individuals who were convinced that God had sent them specifically to lead the truly faithful into the wonderful knowledge and revelations that were sweeping modern Christianity. Faith, confession, shepherding, anointing, submission, speaking the word, demons, deliverance, prosperity and miracles became buzzwords characterizing our particular brand of religion, terms which contributed to isolating us from many having far greater depth and experience. I disagreed with much of what was popular and still do. I experienced rejection and was frustrated with attempts to reconcile what I heard with Who I knew. Not much has changed. I had decided to shut up and enjoy a simple Sunday in a nice church with nice people. Needling the pastor was a side benefit. God was not pleased.

Though the question about the *standard* must remain somewhat unanswered, I do know that I resolved to do what I believed was right in the Lord's sight and to place conforming to the desires of the church authority at a distant second. I decided that conflict with people was of lesser concern than conflict with Him. That's the correct priority.

Shortly after that decision, the Lord directed the reading of the letter.

SOMETIMES I LIKE to compare my Christian life as similar to working for a large company. Jesus used many analogies, which simplify and help us understand more complex concepts. He was often comparing the kingdom of God to some aspect of life to which we can more easily relate.

Following is my analogy, which reveals interesting similarities between church life in a larger sense (as opposed to life in a local church) and a company:

I'm not sure how I got the job with this company, and I'm not sure that I want to work here. I made a commitment to serve the Owner, and apparently at least part of that meant joining His company.

I am absolutely convinced that I know the Owner, and I am usually okay with going along with someone else who also knows the Owner. But there is a lot of activity going on which does not seem to be directly related to the company objective.

To me, it appears that many are using company resources for their own desires, and the Owner, though possibly not pleased, ignores most of it. A few times the Owner has asked me to say some specific things to the employees, which seemed to address some issues, though I thought I could probably do a better job myself. For a few years, I even thought it was my duty to stop some of the nonsense, but the Owner did not back my efforts at any time.

Though I was normally aware of His watchful eye and presence, He seemed to disappear when I went into correction-mode in order to resolve something I found disagreeable. I had even been personally asked by a few employees to attempt to resolve some disputes. I failed consistently and miserably. The Owner was never with me in these attempts and He seemed unconcerned with most of what I saw as violations of company policy.

I like this peculiar Owner, but I don't like or appreciate a lot of the people He has working for Him. Pretty sloppy personnel department, if you ask me, of course.

Most everybody in the company is convinced that they are in on the retirement plan. I'm not sure that a lot of them have even been hired, much less been signed up for the plan. There are people assuming positions and jobs, claiming the Owner has told them something or other, though it often totally conflicts with something someone else claims that the owner has personally told them. What chaos!

I often wonder what the real purpose of the company is. I have heard that the Owner is perfect, not wasteful of resources, knows everything that can be known, and possesses absolute power. Many disagree with the absolute power concept, though. According to some, saying the wrong words can stop the Owner dead in His tracks, which seems silly. That rumor has certainly emboldened many to make some fairly spectacular claims.

I question the true purpose for the company. Though I have been pretty well informed about the accepted purposes of the company by the company management, I also know that managers can be confused about company objectives and can even purposely mislead gullible employees in order to further the manager's own selfish schemes. I've had some firsthand experience with corporate politics.

An obvious company objective, most likely concocted by the human resource department, is to somehow recruit everyone in the world and get them working for the company. Just get their name on an employment contract, seems to be the emphasis. A ton of funds are going toward recruiting. Another stated purpose of the company is to set some sort of universal quality standard. A lot of money is being spent on advertising and lobbying for regulations in an attempt to force the company's quality standards on the marketplace. Little progress is being made there. Seems that few are impressed by the quality of the company's own products. It's easy to spot the company's deficiencies and errors, but what could be right about this organization?

To discover the real purpose for the company, I could work backwards by making some assumptions. If I started with the assumption that the company was actually functioning quite well, despite all of the apparent confusion, what then could be the true objective of the company? What could it be doing so well that the Owner was not the least troubled?

What if the real purpose of the company is as a training ground for the launch of another company? Sure! That would make some sense out of a lot of apparent confusion. Though I could point out the ways the company was not working, I could not think of a better way to train and select the staff for a serious company than to set up a trial one. All of this watching and apparent lack of response by the Owner begins to make some real sense. Sure, there is some real product happening. Smart owners train people on the job. And He steps in at times to sort out a few things, show what He can do and provide a certain amount of interaction with the employees.

But when He really wants something done, it seems that He tells people directly. Even then, the results often seem less important than the willingness of the employee to obey. Some of the orders, even from the Owner, seem to contradict stated company policy, but He seems pleased more by almost blind obedience than by what results from the obedience. Some of the employees occasionally think it necessary to cut a corner or two to achieve a desired result. It's as if they don't truly trust the Owner or understand His ways. All of this struggling for position, this carving out of territory, all of this building of personal fiefdoms.

Why bother? They are obviously unaware of the concurrent separating process. The analogy works quite well for me.

Also, considering those "employees," I often wonder who the group of people is that the Lord was referring to in the following scripture:

> Not everyone who says to Me, "Lord, Lord," will enter the kingdom of heaven; but he who does the will of My Father who is in heaven. Many will say to Me on that day, "Lord, Lord, did we not prophesy in Your name, and in Your name cast out demons, and in Your name perform many miracles?" And then I will declare to them, "I never knew you; depart from Me, you who practice lawlessness." (Matthew 7:21–23)

More on compromise later, but first some more biography.

11
The Gate

The sheer magnitude of the talent often displayed in our church meetings is intimidating to less capable souls who may have only the Lord to offer.

I RECALL A prayer session around 1983. I was on my knees in the rear of a rented house in Grangeville, looking for some serious direction from God. What I was looking for was a sort of heavenly letter spelling out in detail God's exact plan for my life. Once I had that in hand, I planned on following the script exactly, thus securing for me, and hopefully my family, a rosy future and a place in heaven. It was so simple. All I needed was God's will for my life, preferably written on something. Stone would have been perfect.

Though I can't recall the exact circumstances leading up to the particular prayer, I do remember a sense of frustration and desperation. We had quit the logging business, sold the equipment, and I was operating a two-man fabricating shop, building wood-burning stoves on contract for a retailer. The business was not producing enough money.

"Lord, help me. I don't know what to do," I said, looking toward the ceiling.

"Why are you looking up to me?" was the very clear but peculiar response.

"I'm supposed to look to you for guidance and direction to help me make decisions," I replied, fairly surprised at the immediacy and content of His response.

"Look within yourself. I have given you everything you need to make your decision," He said.

"Look within myself?" I thought half out loud.

Look within, inside myself? The answer sounded like something from my New Age days. I knew it was Him, but I couldn't figure this out, and I couldn't ask anyone else. I was already a suspicious character in the minds of several of those presently identified as leaders, and asking what God meant by *look within* would elicit only, "It ain't God."

But I *knew* that it was God, and He was stretching my brain again. Why couldn't He just stick to the Bible, I thought? Keep it simple! Wasn't a child supposed to be able to deal with this stuff? Here I was, approaching forty, no sense of solid direction, and wondering how I was going to support my family now that the logging business was gone. Apparently teaching me some new concept was more important than my personal minor survival issues—food, shelter, etc.

Okay, back to basics. Yes, of course. Psalms 32:8, "I will counsel you with My eye upon you." I recall the above prayer as being one of the first I prayed in looking for general direction in a significant aspect of our lives, such as where we should live or what I should do for a living. Prior to then, our lives had been more like managing crises. I needed more work; we prayed for work and work arrived. Prayers were for immediate needs. At this time, I was considering a new direction for work, even whether I should return to the East Coast to find a job.

God was telling me that I had everything I needed to make a decision, and He expected me to make decisions and accept the responsibility. Supposedly, I had the strength and faith to believe that He was guiding me even though His actual voice was absent. This particular answer contrasted with the then-popular teaching that, if you asked, God would tell you what color Cadillac He preferred that you drive. Okay, I'm exaggerating a little. Not a lot, though.

AS A LOG hauler, I spent considerable time opening and closing gates, lots of gates. Picture driving an eighteen-wheeler loaded with logs down a steep, narrow dirt road and stopping in front of a wire ranch gate; then walking around in front of forty tons of logs and machinery on wheels to open the gate. After opening the gate, I had to drive the truck through and far enough ahead for the end of the load to clear the gate, while trying to minimize the hike back to close the gate and return to the cab of the truck. This all assumed that the brakes held for the procedure. Picture three or four gates times three trips a day in and back out, and time is money.

I conceived of a design for an automatic gate requiring no

electrical power, which would open and close simply by applying limited pressure from the bumper of a vehicle. I knew it would work, but I had no intentions of ever building the contraption. I had little money to build and market such a thing.

In late 1983, I was considering a return to Baltimore to work. During a trip there, God told me to build the gate. I recall actually arguing with Him about it. I had some business sense and knew I was grossly undercapitalized to undertake the venture. He was adamant.

So I built and tested a few prototypes, did a business plan and searched for investors. I made a production run, sold and installed a bunch of gates, and gradually watched the money from the sale of the logging business run out. Finally, by the beginning of 1986, we were broke. With friends paying our rent, I made the decision to head back to Baltimore to find work. The gate project had been a long and frustrating ordeal, culminating in complete failure and embarrassment. My father, during a time of his own frustration, had once said that I was nothing but a bum. Now I had to ask him if we could move in until I could get a job and earn a few paychecks.

At a loading dock, I drove our six-year-old car into the back of a U-Haul and we packed our stuff around it. We piled the rest on a homemade trailer hitched to the back of our seven-year-old four-wheel-drive pickup. Twenty-five hundred miles later, as the four of us prayed, and Cathie and I sorted through our change for gas money in the freezing cold of western Pennsylvania, Jonna looked up at me. She was so small, standing there in the bitter-cold wind.

"Dad?" she asked, shivering.
"What, Jonna?" I answered quickly, distracted by our predicament.
"Are we poor?"

I froze. Her little eyes were looking for hope, but she appeared to be preparing herself to deal with an undesirable conclusion. *Are we poor?* Provision was my responsibility. Had I failed as provider in my daughter's eyes? Was she bracing herself to face the reality that her father was a failure? Was she going to have to abandon her dreams of a secure childhood and accept one of wandering like refugees? Was she thinking that she was going to have to face adulthood before her time and accept her father as being a flawed, barely competent man who had made some very poor choices?

I make no claims about being a good husband or father. I'm not sure a complete definition of a good husband or father actually exists. Like I don't believe that God deals with us through a rule book, I don't like to handle relationships by attempting to conform to a manual. It seems impersonal. I only know that I wanted to do a better job of raising and relating to my children than I thought my father had done. I often felt incompetent and uneasy around my wife and children; like I was under more severe judgment as time went on. It was probably my own delusions. I don't really know.

I never wanted to acknowledge the inadequacies I felt as a father. I thought that pure effort could solve any problem, overcome any obstacle. Sometimes trying harder only makes things worse. When a person tries harder and gets negative feedback, a person can secretly begin to give up. My secret was so deep that I kept it from everyone— even myself.

At that time, the magnitude of our situation was threatening and disheartening. I was older and my resume lacked much significant engineering experience. I knew the chances of getting a good job were reduced, that I might have to settle for something much less than a professional position. What kind of reception awaited us at my parents' home was unknown. I had an engineering degree, brains, excellent health and a family who depended on me. I had been given a ton. So how did we get here, standing in a parking lot in western Pennsylvania, counting quarters, looking like the Beverly Hillbillies, when I had started out with every advantage? Our whole situation descended like an enormous dark cloud about to engulf me and consume all hope for another chance at success. I was frightened. What could I say to her?

"Jonna?"

"Yes?"

"We don't have much money right now, but no, we're not poor. The Lord has a plan. I have an education, I know how to work, and I will find a good job. We will find a house, and you will be okay." I crouched down to look into her eyes and said, "Okay?"

"Thanks, Dad," she said with obvious relief.

"Okay," I said to myself as I stood back up. She believed me. I wasn't so sure I did.

Now in order to market the automatic gate, I had a professional color brochure printed. The era was before inexpensive printing became common. I was proud of it and carried that brochure along with my resume on my job interviews. I interviewed for everything from piano sales to forensics. Fortunately, within a reasonable time I was hired for an engineering position by a manufacturing firm south of Baltimore.

My boss, who interviewed me for the job, later told me the details of how I got hired. He said that when I first entered his office for the interview, something or someone told him to hire me. He knew I was the man for the job immediately. However, the president of the company, who had to approve engineering hires, resisted. He had felt that, having been a logger, I was not qualified. My boss said that he then showed the brochure to the president. That gate brochure clinched the job.

What do you suppose the real purpose for the gate was? Who do you suppose told an unbeliever to hire me? God had a three-year plan to get me back into the profession for which I was educated. Is God cool or what? Give Him the glory.

SHORTLY AFTER BEING hired by the company, I was asked to make a compromise. I was given an illegal copy of a software package to use for my work in obtaining a patent on a product we were developing. The company had simply bought a single copy, made additional copies of the disks and manuals and distributed them to any employee needing the software. It seemed ironic that they would ask me to use stolen intellectual property to protect their intellectual property from theft.

"I can't use this," I said.

"Why? What's the problem?" my boss asked.

"It's bootlegged software. I don't use stolen software or equipment to do a job," I replied. "I don't steal my food or clothes either." I needed the job, but I knew what happened when I compromised, and this was blatant. God was watching.

My boss was perplexed. He probably realized that firing me would have been a bad idea. I might contact the software company, who would be delighted to have a juicy piracy report. The issue simmered for a few weeks. I avoided the subject and managed to get on with other work. In the meantime, while browsing a trade magazine, I spotted an ad for a cheap software package that I thought I could use to do the job. It was only around fifty dollars compared to over three thousand for the real thing. I had some personal use for the product, so I bought it. I began using it and found that I could do the company's work with it. My boss was relieved. So was I. Good deal.

Word of the incident spread and it must have dawned on the president that the copying policy was exposing his company to serious litigation. He eventually broke down and had legal copies purchased.

AS A FAMILY, we prayed every night before we went to bed.

"Lord, please let us move back to Idaho," Jonna would often say, as the four of us knelt along our bed. "We really miss being there."

Later, I would sometimes remind her, "That's nice that you would like to return to Idaho, but we live in Baltimore now. Idaho is in the past. We have to learn to be happy here and look ahead. Okay?"

"Yeah, but is it still okay if I just ask?" she replied one time.

"You can always ask whatever you would like to ask. It's fine with me."

"Thanks, Dad. And I'll try to be happy here in Maryland," she said, looking down. "Dad?" Jonna asked, looking back up.

"Yes, Jonna?"

"Do you know why I like you?"

"Why?"

"Because you always make me feel better."

I worked there for four years. By late winter in 1990, I began getting strange feelings as I entered my office at the company. It was like I was not going to be there much longer. During an awkward conversation with my boss, I asked him about it.

"I'm not going to be here for long, am I?"

"Uh, I'm not sure … uh," he stuttered.

"It's okay. I know I'm gone. Am I right?" I insisted.

"How did you know? There are some general layoffs coming

because the project you're working on is done. I wanted to tell you myself, but who told you?"

"God, I guess," I replied. "It's okay. I've known for a few weeks that it was time to move on."

I liked my boss. He and I had become friends, but I was not in the mix at the company. They were very generous with the separation package. I spread my resume up and down the East Coast. With zero responses, I extended my search to the Northwest and drove there to look for opportunities. They were still working on getting the Internet fully up, so finding jobs was a manual project.

I managed an interview with a company in eastern Washington, and while hanging around, I stopped by a commercial realtor to see if any interesting businesses were for sale. We had remodeled our Baltimore house and the market was skyrocketing. With the severance package and the potential sale of our home, I figured I had enough money to invest in a small business.

"Howdy. What's going on?" an agent asked as I walked into a downtown Spokane realtor's office.

"Not a lot. Any small businesses available?" I said.

"A few. What type are you looking for?"

"Something involving metal or equipment."

"So, where are you from, if I might ask?"

"Baltimore."

"Long ways. Well, here's a couple to look at. I also have one that's pretty remote. I suppose you wouldn't be interested in living in a very small town."

"I might. Tell me about it," I said.

"It's a small manufacturing business about one hundred and fifty miles south of here, in Cottonwood, Idaho, just north of Grangeville."

"So 'Bill' is selling, huh?" I said, naming the business owner, to the realtor's surprise.

"What? How do you know him? I mean, you're from Baltimore, right?"

"I moved from Grangeville to Baltimore four years ago. This business used to make parts for a product I sold for a short time," I informed him, enjoying his amazement. God was *clearly* at work again.

Sometimes He's so, like, totally obvious. It is astonishing how people can continue to deny His existence. Who or what else could orchestrate all of this stuff?!

I drove south to Cottonwood to see my friend from the past, and worked out a deal. I could only afford half of the business, so we decided on a partnership agreement. I called my wife, and she agreed. She put the house on the market. It sold quickly for a nice profit, which together with the severance package was just enough to purchase my share of the business, move us back to Grangeville and make a small down payment on another house. We needed the first paycheck, but we were happy. I thought we were happy.

"Hey, Dad, guess what?" Anna would often say.
"What?" I'd ask.
"That's what," she'd reply.
"You got me again," I confessed. It's hard when you begin to think that your daughters might be smarter than you are. Apparently Jonna was at least a better prayer.

Yeah, we all knew that God had brought us back to the place we loved. This time, though, I had some absolutely direct, relevant industry experience, which would prove invaluable in transforming a small job shop into a high tech money-making machine.

Was it the faith and persistent prayer of a small child that did the trick? It was a mystery to me.

COMPROMISE COMES CLOAKED in disguises sophisticated enough to fool even the most astute observer, as I thought of myself. And I did think of myself more and more as we progressed into the nineties. Work was exciting and challenging. Gradually the profits began to appear and to increase. We were able to afford college educations for our children, a new home on some acreage and lots of additional comforts.

There is a quote from a character in *Pogo*, a popular comic strip I used to read, which is, "We have met the enemy, and he is us." After a few years of success, my carnal self, in a way, seemed to have figured out my spiritual self. That is, I seemed to say something like this, "Okay, I have this Christian deal pretty well figured out now. Thank you, Lord, but I can handle things from here on. I see what this is all about. Yes, I'll go through most of the obligatory Christian motions, but I see the plan clearly enough now to figure the rest out. I'll let you know if anything needs your attention." Sound bad? It probably wasn't that bad, although maybe it was worse.

It's hard to judge the true height of the trees from so deep in the woods.

I had developed a new two-part attitude. The first part, which I'll call the Christian part, of my new attitude is best described in a conversation with a guy from a Monday morning men's group I attended shortly after my eventual move to Coeur d'Alene. The group is described later. This very vocal friend was going on and on about some revelation of his, and complaining about the church leadership, or something about how they didn't appreciate his input. He was pushy. I could easily relate.

I said, "Brother?"

"What?" he asked.

"Sometimes you just need to shut up."

"Huh?"

"Shut up. You know. Keep quiet. Listen. You'd be surprised."

"But, God has shown me some things …!"

"Maybe, but you're running over the top of everyone, mowing them down with all this stuff. You're good, very good, but you can be *too* good. Sometimes it's better to keep a lower profile."

"What do you mean?"

"Got a minute for a little story?" I asked.

"I guess," he replied.

"Well, maybe five or so years ago I was quite the thing, at least according to me. I held Bible studies at my house. We began with my playing the piano while we sang some scripture or worship songs and then moved into a discussion or scripture study, both led by me. There were a few complaints about the fact that I was usually doing everything, so I encouraged others to lead the worship or study or whatever. But rarely did anyone else actually take the initiative."

"Why?" he asked.

So I explained it the way the Lord presented it to me. The rebuke was possibly not quite as stinging as the following words imply, but God basically said, *"Who could do anything with you around? You play the piano, you teach the Bible, guide the discussions, challenge people's faith, and now you have more money than everybody else. You're intimidating. Why would anybody else feel comfortable presenting what they had?"*

"Wow," was the best he could say.

"Pretty ugly, huh?"

"Yeah. I mean, sorry or ..."

"That's all right," I said. "God whacked me off just above the knees."

The second aspect of my new attitude was related to financial independence. I never gave a lot of thought to our financial future until about the middle of the nineties. I was always busy with immediate crises and trying to get some sort of reasonable income to happen. Suddenly, the possibility of actually planning for retirement with some resources appeared, having surfaced almost imperceptibly.

What was *this* that I was staring at? Could we actually think about retiring in fifteen or so years with enough to live on in reasonable comfort? I had seldom thought of our lives as middle class, but there we were. The thought occurred to me that if I could quickly get into some serious planning and hoarding, or rather investing, we might arrive at retirement with substantial resources. Visions of a little business in some resort area floated around in our heads, along with traveling in a nice motor home—a modest one, of course.

Life gave every appearance of being under the control of my grimy little paws. Planning was made on the basis of financial gain, geographical preference and social mix, with little serious consideration as to what God, who had made all of those options a real possibility, might have in mind for our future.

PERHAPS I COULD have looked up and seen the storm brewing in the clouds on the horizon. Perhaps I could have remembered the words He had spoken to me regarding a specific purpose He had prepared. Maybe I could have listened to the deafening silence which permeated my stagnant spiritual life. Maybe I might have seen that my wife was becoming increasingly disenchanted with me, and I would have cried out to Him earlier.

But I didn't. No. It was like I was back at that church, back to pleasing only myself, compromised to the max—that was, until that drive to work in 2001 around Crays' corner when I uttered that critical prayer.

Hindsight is so good. Though in some ways I probably knew better, I doubt I could have done things differently. We make the choices we do because of who we are, not because of what we know. Who among us has not committed sins knowing we shouldn't? Even Paul declared that sin operated within him, causing him to do that which he knew he should not. No, God must deliver us from ourselves—literally change us from within. Simple knowledge won't cut it.

KNOWLEDGE, AS FACTS, is a powerful tool, which God has afforded us to use in functioning in the finite world we are born into. It is, however, imperfect. To lean very much at all upon factual knowledge is to merely skirt true relationship with our Creator.

P. D. Ouspensky wrote a novel entitled, *The Strange Life of Ivan Osokin*. In this imaginary tale, Ivan was given the chance by a carnival gypsy to live his flawed life over again with full knowledge of his previous life. He assumed that knowledge of his past errors would enable him to avoid making the same grievous mistakes. He was unsuccessful. Though he was fully aware of the consequences of his actions, he made the same choices. He did what he did because he was who he was, not because of what he knew as facts.

Knowledge, even sound Biblical knowledge, can be a dangerously false god. To assume that through knowledge and understanding we can accomplish God's purposes is arrogance and vanity. God must change us from within, make us into His new creation and accomplish His purpose Himself. It takes time and it's not automatic. He does the work and deserves the credit. We get the benefits.

12

Charlotte

There exists within many mature males (and presumably females) a fundamental need to fix things. That need, when combined with scriptural knowledge, can result in an annoying tendency to apply the "word of God" in the most inappropriate situations with a callousness exceeding that of school children.

IN OCTOBER 2006, I decided to relocate to Charlotte, North Carolina. To some, heading for Charlotte appeared to be another random decision on my part. They implied that I was running from my problems. *Wherever you go, there you are.* Cute.

I believed that Charlotte was where God wanted me. I cannot explain how I know such things. Sometimes the Lord uses a combination of my basic common sense, natural tendencies, attitude, fears and anxieties, prevailing weather conditions, and Biblical knowledge to guide me. I'll explain.

Basic common sense: With my house sold and my furniture tucked safely in a storage unit, I assessed my situation. I had no reason to believe that the Lord wanted me to do anything but work. Though jobs or businesses in which to invest were probably available in the Northwest, my Internet research had revealed a more target-rich environment in the Southeast.

Natural tendencies and attitude: I work. I've always worked. If I was raised wrong, fine. It is tiresome to read and hear that there is some perfect person we are supposed to be, provided we are raised correctly. There is certainly value in undoing the lies and denials of reality which can result from childhood trauma, but God made us a certain way, and part of that making is how we were raised. I think He made me the way I am and actually likes me that way. Maybe He *prefers* me that way. Sure, I have some attitude and I tend to push boundaries. Maybe Western Christianity needs some boundary pushing, and I don't mind doing a little bit of it.

Fears and anxieties: The thought of facing another typical winter of Northwest rain and dark clouds was literally frightening to me. I could no longer stay in a rented room, watch the rain pour down and be confined to the indoors. I needed sunshine.

Prevailing weather conditions: The winter weather in the Southeast is normally much friendlier, with lots of pleasant sun.

Biblical knowledge: As a principle, it is not wise to invest in a house without a business or job secured first. Here is the scripture:

Prepare your work outside, And make it ready for yourself in the field; Afterwards, then, build your house. (Proverbs 24:27)

Charlotte seemed to pop into my brain when I pictured the Southeast. I wasn't sure why, though it certainly was fairly central to my job/business search. I also had occasional contact with a couple, James and Rhonda Tomasi, I'd known from Coeur d'Alene. I understood they traveled in ministry almost constantly, and I thought that their quarters were probably temporary. I noticed from their Web site that they were based in Charlotte. I e-mailed them and promised to call when I arrived. With enough stuff for an extended stay loaded in my pickup truck, I drove across the country.

I OCCASIONALLY FEEL anxiety from watching my bank account dwindle. Having made very little money in recent years, and with nothing immediately in sight, I often resort to saving a few dollars by sleeping in questionable motels. You would think that having been through several financial crises and always coming out okay, that I would relax. Not so. As time goes on, I occasionally still find it difficult to face some situations. If that which does not kill us only makes us stronger, then nothing I have faced must have been actually life-threatening. At times I seem remarkably unable to simply ignore insignificant threats to my well-being.

My first day in Charlotte, I awoke and saw a roach on the wall in my motel room. The whole time I lived in the Northwest, I never saw a roach. I've heard that if you see one, you are not seeing its thousand friends nearby.

I don't mind noisy crowds, but I like peace and quiet in my home. I love to get muddy and sweaty during some exhilarating outdoor activity, but I like a clean shower afterwards. I'm not afraid of bugs, but I prefer not to sleep with them. I prefer to sleep in a reasonably clean environment. It's a control thing, I guess.

I left the motel in a hurry but had to pull off the side of the road to cry. I'd been crying a lot for nearly five years, and besides the sobbing, the episodes would include some emotional and mental disintegration. It is not a pretty sight. Recovery from the episodes is slow. It requires clear thinking and assessing of my true situation and occasionally takes more energy than I'm able to muster. At such times, the kind intervention of considerate, close friends is required for reasonable progress.

I still occasionally have such breakdowns, and I have some idea how to avoid most of them. Among other things, it is important not to be alone for too long, to wallow in self-pity, or to be around my relatives too much with their happy families and grandchildren. And I must avoid cheap motels.

Crying in the morning wrecks the whole day. I've started businesses, machine designs, houses, fights, games, machinery, cars and trucks, meetings, songs, running, arguments, boats and Humvees, among many other things. I've never started any of those things by crying. Apparently we start life by crying. Maybe I have this backwards, too, but crying did not seem like a good way to start life in another new town. No, I had to find a better way to begin life in Charlotte.

So, I dried my eyes and decided to call my friends, James and Rhonda. I was totally surprised to find them delighted that I had come. They quickly offered me temporary quarters in a spare room in their comfortable townhouse, and generally helped to lift my spirits immensely. God was there again. He showed up in remarkable ways confirming that Charlotte was the right place. It was clearly the next stone on which to place my foot. I was still on His narrow road and He was still watching, guiding, orchestrating and providing

A COUPLE OF weeks after arriving in Charlotte, I was standing in front of the sink in the Tomasis' home contemplating upper cervical (UC) chiropractic which addresses a particular region of the spine in our necks. James and Rhonda are advocates of UC care and spend a great deal of time involved with UC practitioners, traveling and speaking on their behalf. They are very excited about UC manipulation and tell me often of the healings witnessed, which is surprising considering the relative simplicity of the procedure.

Many healings appear to be absolutely supernatural. James, who has a remarkable story to tell about his own healing from trigeminal neuralgia, always manages to work God into his presentations. And God seems to use him in His work. Why? What was the big deal with UC? Why did God appear to be so involved in this seemingly simple UC work?

"I can use that," was all He said as I stood there at the sink.

There He was again, I thought. Another simple sentence that fell like a seed into the soil of my mind, where it germinated, took immediate root, shot up into the light and formed a huge tree with branches everywhere. Why do His words do that? Why is there so much life in what He says, and yet we can be so boring? James once told me about a pastor who claimed God had informed him, *"You should talk more about Me than about you. I'm much more interesting than you are."* Exactly. God is so rich.

So now those simple words began to grow in my mind into another dialogue, but first a little background on James.

I MET JAMES in Coeur d'Alene the fall of 2003. Approaching two years since my wife had left, I was still in rough shape. "Come and join our Monday morning men's group," James, then an associate pastor, said insistently. I needed someone to insist. I needed some friends badly, but I was poor at starting friendships, having made little progress over my youth. Now I was no longer so self-sufficient, so self-confident. I needed help. James befriended me and asked me to join a bunch of men who met each Monday at seven o'clock in the morning. The men gathered to relate personal experiences and emotions. It was one of those bonding things.

I didn't like to be around lots of men. What was it? Too much aftershave, testosterone or bull? Whichever it was, the aftershave was there in the morning, and I was worried that the bull was waiting. Testosterone is great in physical competition, but I was easily annoyed by it in conversation. Men are fixers, and I'd had my fill of attempts at repair. I said that I would come, but I wanted a low profile, which was unacceptable to James.

"Tell your story. It will be good for you. You're the speaker for next Monday," I heard after a few Mondays. I was not interested and managed to maneuver through several weeks of being the featured guy without dumping my tale on twenty-five dangerous men. It wasn't that I was afraid of them; I was afraid of my probable response to what I figured would be their response. I was tired of and becoming irritated by scriptures and platitudes. I had heard them too many times in just a year and a half of being on the injured list, a list I was never on before; that is, in my previous life as a husband, business owner and all that. Now I wasn't sure who I was, and that's not a secure position from which to face a group I viewed as harboring many testosterone-loaded minister wannabes.

"Tell your story, or do you want to listen while I tell it myself?" James insisted. That could be worse. I would sit there like a mouse and what credibility I had left would be trampled immediately. All right, I would face the hoards, but with conditions.

"Good morning, men," I said. "James has asked me to tell you my situation, so I will. I do ask one thing before I begin, and that is, no advice after I'm finished. Please. No more platitudes, reminders of Romans 8:28, other scripture verses, assurances that everything is going to be rosy, or that you've been there and know how I feel. No offense, but I'm filled up to the eyeballs with all of that. More of the same is just wasting breath." It was easy to see that my legendary friend-making skills were being employed at maximum strength.

So, I told them my tale. Afterwards, one kind man asked what they, as a group, could do. Excellent, I thought. Here is a reasonable and considerate man. It wasn't so bad. I might live.

"Pray for me," I replied, "and let me come here and listen. Thank you."

I did go many times after that, and I did listen. There were wonderful moments when men confessed their sins, expressed their fears and received wise counsel. But still, I frequently observed some speaking into others' lives in an intrusive and authoritative or condescending manner.

What possesses us that we feel the need to offer such often pathetic advice, advice which appears almost demeaning, so patronizing? Is it that the suffering individual is in such a vulnerable position that our primal need to assert dominance cannot be restrained? Or is it that not having something supposedly profound to say makes us look inept and helpless when someone is in such obvious pain?

I have experienced both tender care and callous responses to the awareness of my pain. Kindness flows from those who have truly experienced life-altering trauma, shattering events from which recovery is never complete. Their observance of my pain must remind them of their own time of difficulty, and their internal caution lamp lights.

"Be careful," Wisdom must be warning them. "Remember how fragile you were. Resist the temptation to qualify yourself, to show that you have relevant knowledge and to diminish the other person's pain to a level you assume you can handle with confidence. Think, or even better, pray, before you say anything. Perhaps the person is suffering for the Lord. God is, no doubt, watching how you handle this. He may or may not be pleased with what you say or do. Your words will indicate whom you are interested in pleasing. This could be a mini-test to see if you are worthy to rise to the level of the one standing in front of you, the one who is in such pain."

BACK IN CHARLOTTE, as I was standing in front of the sink, the Lord said about UC, *"I can use that."*

Being a person who prefers function over appearance, I like to see purpose or connection. I go to the doctor and I take medicine. Some chemicals interact and the medicine does its work. I assume that if God isn't going to heal me supernaturally, I'm okay with natural or synthetic methods. I just want to be well. I have so often made a distinction between natural and supernatural that I've failed to see Him in more places.

I don't want to attribute words to God that aren't from Him, so the following is somewhat hypothetical. It is another transfer of thoughts, but I believe it to be what He was conveying to me regarding His words, *I can use that.*

I responded with, "Really? You can use UC? What do you mean by that?"

"I use lots of stuff. It's really all me, Jonathan. You fail to acknowledge that."

"All you?"

Yes. I use all sorts of things, even though you don't acknowledge the connection. In addition to UC, I can use doctors, drugs, mud, spit, water, and jackasses. I can use anything, but I choose what I use."

"Choose what you use?"

"No guarantee that I will use anything, no matter how perfect or imperfect it may appear. I may choose to use a TV evangelist or an unbelieving general of a heathen army to perform my will.

"Even you set criteria for what is acceptable. Too often you differentiate between the natural and supernatural. You think it's either natural or supernatural. You think that if I am not going to do something supernatural, then natural means will suffice. I use it all. I'm in everything. It pleases me to show up in places people don't expect me to. I've cautioned you about having expectations. My people have many of the wrong expectations of Me and are suffering from wounds and doubts as a result. I've even asked you to write a book, and your immediate response is to wonder what use that could be, with all of the books already written. You think that everything that could be said has been said many times over. What could you add?

"What does it matter? I've asked you to write a book. Write it, and perhaps I will use it. I may use it for something, but perhaps not what you expect. Remember that word?"

"Expectations. Expectations are the source of many frustrations."

"I can use anything. That's My choice. I expect the best from My sons. That's good stewardship, responsible use of the talents and gifts I have given them. Like anyone else, you should use your abilities with discretion. Whether I choose to use your efforts supernaturally, naturally, or not at all is My choice. I can use anything.

"Do you remember the mother and daughter who sang for Me at the little Pentecostal church in Kooskia shortly after you were first saved, how you wanted to leave because they started singing so badly?"

"Yes, yes. I figured they were going to be awful."

"Do you remember how I anointed their singing and how you were stunned?"

"I was stunned. Yes, You; they were astonishing."

"Do you remember the crummy pianos?"

"Yes." I was thinking, remembering.

"I can use that."

DIVORCE AFTER A long marriage is somewhat like being exiled to a foreign country called "Singleland." Though it occupies the same geographical area as "Marriedland," Singleland has its own culture, idioms, and customs. I know people who like to travel to foreign countries, who dream of living someday in a foreign country and who would possibly flourish in some foreign culture. Personally I like the U.S., and I prefer Marriedland to Singleland. Some married people I have talked to see Singleland as a cool place and express some envy regarding my new citizenship. Perhaps to them married life is dull or pointless. Singleland ain't that great. Believe me.

And I'm sure that, to many people accustomed to life in larger metropolitan areas, life in rural Idaho can seem dull or pointless. I knew of, and have heard stories about, couples who moved to rural parts of Idaho, built a nice house on some ridge overlooking one of the beautiful rivers, stayed a few months and left. They didn't get it, I guess.

That's okay. The Lord made people different, diverse, and we don't have to see life the same way, live in the same places, like the same things, or agree on very much at all. In Ephesians 4:13 Paul teaches that we are becoming unified in faith—not necessarily in fleshly preferences.

That's a good thing. Can you imagine how miserable life would be if we all agreed on everything? Think about it. I never gave much real thought to diversity until I was relocated to Singleland.

"How many of you like diversity?" I once heard a preacher in nearly totally white North Idaho ask his congregation. I raised my hand, though I saw few other hands go up.

"I'm for diversity," I said under my breath.

"Well, I'm personally very glad that God created diversity," he went on. "There isn't a *guy* in the world I'd want to be married to."

"Very good," I said quietly. "I like that."

Throughout nature, we can observe the benefits of diversity in strengthening ecosystems, and balancing or limiting the tendency for one species to dominate. Even in market systems, diversity and competition play a crucial role in lowering prices and raising product and service quality. We all agree to this, don't we? None of us would like our competitors to sort of disappear, right? Of course. So how well does diversity play out in our Christian experience?

My true position on diversity is somewhat complex. I was raised in a white suburb of northern Baltimore, listening to my father's complaints about how the African Americans were taking over the city where his business was located. I do not want to be disrespectful to my father or anyone else, but he referred to them as n------s. It was strange to hear, because my father was not an actual bigot. He was insecure, felt threatened, and became defensive. He may have been correct in perceiving a need to defend his inner-Baltimore business property from value deterioration or vandalism, but the blame was misplaced. I will discuss later that God can use our defensive behavior to expose our prejudices and worse—idols we may have created.

While I was in high school, I worked at my father's business for a few summers with some of his black employees. I could tell that they genuinely liked him and he liked them, which contrasted with what I often heard at the dinner table. My father, who seemed to have conflicting perceptions, was not above hiring a questionable guy from the streets who sometimes got into legal trouble and needed help. My dad helped. My dad, like a lot of us, was okay as long as he didn't feel threatened.

Personally, I had little to fear from the African Americans I was around, except when I walked home from wrestling practice during dark, winter evenings. The alternative technical high school I attended was surrounded mostly by black folks and I used public transportation commuting to and from school. I worried a bit, walking alone to the bus stop on dark evenings, but I also worried about walking through many white areas. Though actual gangs were not common, neighborhood bullies and their friends were.

When I arrived in Idaho, I noticed that the Native Americans appeared to me to represent the "feared minority." Few African Americans lived in Idaho. Though I'm certainly simplifying, I concluded that the Native Americans were the regional perceived threat, perhaps since it was assumed that they were unfairly using public money, must be lazy and might move in next door. I often examined my own position, wondering how I would react if I were in a position of feeling threatened by someone of color. For me, skin color is not the factor. Culture is the factor. It isn't the color of a man's skin which I possibly find threatening, it's the color of his culture. I imagine there are blind racists. I don't truly know.

American churches have a history of missions to foreign countries. I have admiration for the thousands who have dedicated their lives to preaching the gospel to the world. Some of that is marred, though, by occasional attempts to enforce our culture along with the gospel presentation. I doubt that God is more pleased by Western-style worship. Think about that for a minute. Think about the various forms of worshiping God taking place among all the different cultures in the world. Now consider how often the form of worship in our church meetings is the subject of contention and strife. How open to diversity are we?

As a once-married and presently single man, it has taken a long time for me to realize that many of my fears and anxieties stem significantly from having been forced into an unknown "culture" where I have little or no control over my life, and I feel somewhat threatened by the diversity surrounding me. I felt much safer and more insulated from the pain of others in my nice house, surrounded by my familiar family and friends. Yet that present lack of control has become a source of riches I could not have received any other way. Though I may resent having to endure these experiences, I cannot deny the richness of their diversity.

We would do well to allow more spiritual diversity in our church life, to let God be larger, to abandon our spiritual neighborhoods and to allow input from those He sends to us from different spiritual cultures. We might then allow Him to richen our experiences.

Single people represent the majority of our population, yet church life is predominantly married-with-family based. The stigma associated with divorce routinely negatively affects decisions regarding leadership and qualifications. Single people, among others, are discriminated against. Church leaders may deny such discrimination, but denial doesn't remove the problem. The issue remains. Ask around Singleland.

We should loosen the standards some/many have imposed as a type of filter to screen out supposedly objectionable intrusions. Are we willing to allow God to enhance our lives through diverse experiences?

THOUGH I CAN acknowledge the benefits of spiritual diversity, there remains within me the desire to return to a neighborhood more familiar. I, too often, resent the continual challenge to rise higher in faith. Pain again becomes apparent when I'm reminded of my former life, when I had a "life."

Fall 2006, and my cell phone rang.

"Brad."

"Hi, Jonathan. What's up?"

"Oh, just driving north along Interstate 81 in Virginia, headed for my sister's house and the annual Christmas get-together with the rels."

"Are you looking forward to it?"

"I guess. I enjoy seeing them, but the Christmas season is rough. I see my friends and relatives with their families and grandchildren, and me alone, and, well, you know."

"Yeah, I imagine that the Christmas season is difficult for a lot of people. You're going to be okay, brother. He's going to bless you. It will be a real testimony."

"You know, Brad, I'm really tired of hearing that. I love you, man, and I know you don't really understand what I'm dealing with, so I'm just asking you to stop saying that, okay?"

"Hey. You know, some people wouldn't mind being like you, free to do whatever they want, not tied down to a routine. Man, you can live anywhere, probably pick any place and find something. You're not that old. You're healthy, no bills. Must have a few bucks. Sounds not too bad to me."

"Get off it, Brad. Would you like to trade places with me?"

"Uh, well, not really ..."

"Why not?"

"Well, I've got obligations. You know. My wife, kids. Stuff."

"Gee, for a minute it sounded like not having those would be great. I guess not having those is great for me, but not for you, huh?"

"Well, that's not what I meant."

"Actually, I think it is. Listen, Brad. You're not one of those people who would go to some foreign country, look around at all of the squalor, and try to convince the poor souls that they really had it pretty good so you could go back home, sit in your great room, watch your big-screen TV and feel justified, are you?"

"Hey, man, you're upset, and maybe we should talk later."

"Why? What's wrong with now? Why avoid me when I start to

address difficult issues as if it's always a problem *I* have? Why do you try to smooth things over with some pathetic platitude? You got a minute?"

"Uh, not really. I was …"

"Let me lay something out for *you*, brother. Five years ago I had a family, nice house, a business, a retirement, things to do and places to go. I had a life. I put my children through college. I worked my butt off for years. I lived as right as I could live. I rarely went anywhere without my family. Sure, I wasn't perfect. Sure, I knew my wife wasn't totally happy. I knew I wasn't the greatest catch, but there were worse husbands. People have admitted that.

"I asked my wife, begged her to show me a better husband, but she couldn't, or wouldn't. I've been to divorce care, counseling sessions, deliverance ministry, seminars; you name it. I've heard stories of families sticking together through affairs, abuse, sickness and all kinds of financial disaster. There are some really wonderful people out there who have proven, time and again, that blood truly *is* thicker than water; amazing people who have made their marriage vows the theme for their lives.

"You show me, dear brother, show me exactly what I did, what sin I committed, what grave error precipitated this whole sequence of events that caused me to go from where I was to living alone in a rented bedroom, with no job, having to drug myself to sleep; livin' like a flippin' college student at my age."

Hearing only silence, I asked, "Well?"

"I have no idea," Brad finally replied.

"What?"

"I don't know."

"Don't know what? What sin it was? You can't get it out of your brain, can you? You have to believe that there must have been something I did to cause this catastrophe. Right?"

"I'm sorry, Jonathan. I'm truly sorry that this all happened, but things don't happen without reason."

"Actually, they do, Brad, and here is why you refuse to accept that."

"Why?"

"Because, then it could happen to you."

"What do you mean?"

"I said that it could happen to you."

"I don't understand."

"God might do the *same thing to you*! It's like hell, brother. People think that not believing in hell means that they will never end up there. It's the height of denial. Though you can't identify the cause, the connection between my actions and what resulted, you're sure it's there. It must be there. It has to be there. You're sure there must be something you do, your lifestyle, something you believe or confess that separates you from people like me. Otherwise . . ."

"Otherwise, what?"

"Otherwise, it could happen to you! Your life would be out of your control. *Anything* could happen! God might come in and destroy the whole thing right before your eyes. You think that you have God figured out. You think that by living a certain way, praying certain ways, confessing certain things, or reading the right books, that you will be spared the disaster you see when you see me.

"You worship a god who makes you feel *comfortable* with him, who does only good things, a *user-friendly* god, predictable and innocuous. Is *any* of this getting through to you?"

"I don't know what to say."

"What?"

"I don't know. I don't know what to say. I care about you a lot, but I just don't know what to say or do. I pray for you often. I hate to see you hurting."

"Thank you."

"Huh?"

"That's the best thing you could say."

"I'm missin' it here, bro."

"That's even better. Brad, you don't have to understand. You *can't* understand, and that's okay. Sometimes things happen, and they can happen anytime to anyone. Sometimes there's a reason, sometimes not. Do you remember the story of the man born blind?" I asked.

"Yeah. The Lord said that no one sinned. Okay, I hear you."

"Do you hear me?"

"I think I do, maybe."

"Brother, I'm getting to like you. I've been having to love you all of this time, but now, yeah, I think I like you."

"Can I ask you a question?" Brad said.

"Fire away."

"How come you get so down sometimes? Christmas is pretty bad, huh?"

"Real bad. I go to see my family. I see their grandchildren, their lives, their joy and happiness, and I realize what I lost. That's all. There are a lot of people for whom Christmas is a rough time. The reality is that it can be a financially and emotionally traumatic time for many people. You don't see them? I hardly thought about them when I had a life. I see lots of them now, hanging out on the edges, in the shadows, like people who missed their train."

"I'll keep that in mind."

"Do that. Thanks again."

"Do you feel like you missed your train?" Brad asked after some delay.

"Sometimes, but not really. No, here's what I have to believe. I missed one train or fell off or whatever, but there's another coming. I don't know the train schedule, but there has to be more than one train on these tracks. I'm sure of it. These tracks are too well used. Besides, the truth is, unlike some others, I haven't ridden the same train all of my life. I don't know why some people seem to ride only one or two trains in their lives. I feel like I've ridden several, so there is probably another on the way. I do wonder what that one will be like, but right now I have no idea."

"So what are you going to do?"

"Keep walking and listening, I guess."

"For the next train."

"Yeah, I guess. That too."

"A lot of people are praying for you, you know. You have a lot of friends."

"I know, and that's not normal."

"What, bro?"

"Having a lot of friends. I've never had so many friends, people who care, who call me and ask how I am."

"We're your family, buddy. You know what they say?"

"Yes, I know. You can choose your friends, but you can't choose your family."

"You got it. You're stuck with us."

He was right. So I spent time with my brother and sisters, nieces and nephews, cousins and all, saw their grandchildren, and caught up with what everybody was doing. A few asked some polite questions. I gave some answers. After so many years, most know what not to ask. It was an emotional time. They are warm, fun people, and they are living their lives, paying bills, making plans, comparing pictures of children, grandchildren and birthday parties, and updating news about friends. I stayed a couple of days and headed back to Charlotte. I really tried not to cry. Doggone it.

ANOTHER CONVERSATION, IN the shower, of course, at James' place.

"I'm teaching you something," He began. These were not words, but impressions that were gentler, hanging around in the air for plucking, like the ripe, tantalizing fruit of a wondrous tree.

In the last nearly five years, I'd said horrible things to God, wanted to run anywhere to get away from Him, felt the worst loneliness and rejection, and blamed it all on Him. Yet when He shows up, I can't resist Him. He becomes my desire. His words fill the air I breathe. His Spirit, like a clean wind, blows through me sweeping away every trace of accumulated clutter and debris.

"Take some, if you want," the words seemed to beckon, not forcing themselves, but merely tempting me to taste and see. They floated nearer, engulfing me. I tasted.

"I'm teaching you something," they whispered.

"I think I know already, Lord." The tears flowed freely. He was a light misty cloud above me.

"Do you love me, Jonathan?"

"You know the answer, but I can't say it right now. Please don't ask me. Not right now."

"I'm teaching you something."

"Yes, I know."

"Unconditional love."

"I know. Lesson two."

"Do you love me?"

"I'm not able …"

"Do you love me, Jonathan?"

13

The Two Golden Calves

One way that an object, concept, doctrine or institution can be exposed as an idol is by its worshiper's vigorous defense. The extent to which people display offense to criticism of their religious doctrines, churches, character, or accomplishments, for example, can be a measure of the idol such things may have become to them. If God, who does not even defend Himself, is truly our source, our means, and our end, why spend energy defending from mere criticism that which will perish anyway?

YEARS AGO THE Lord began to speak to me about two golden calves. I was not yet familiar with any passage about two golden calves, though the words were before me like actual text. I recall that only periodically did He draw my attention to the phrase, but eventually He indicated a particular verse. The context of the verse is that Solomon has died, and Israel has been divided between his two sons, Jeroboam and Rehoboam. Judah was separated from the remaining tribes, but the temple was in Jerusalem, in Judah.

Then Jeroboam built Shechem in the hill country of Ephraim, and lived there. And he went out from there and built Penuel. And Jeroboam said in his heart, "Now the kingdom will return to the house of David. If this people go up to offer sacrifices in the house of the LORD at Jerusalem, then the heart of this people will return to their lord, even to Rehoboam king of Judah; and they will kill me and return to Rehoboam king of Judah." So the king consulted, and made two golden calves, and he said to them, "It is too much for you to go up to Jerusalem; behold your gods, O Israel, that brought you up from the land of Egypt." And he set one in Bethel, and the other he put in Dan. (1 Kings 12:25–29)

One of the ways I test the words from God is to watch the words, feel the words, and try to grasp their essence. Do they sit solidly in my soul, and instead of being weakened by every scriptural challenge I can muster, actually reveal some subtle concept obviously spread throughout the pages of my Bible? When I question His words, He sends little examples with reminders attached like printed labels, which help to sort through and order which phrase or concept belongs with what. Gradually a clear picture emerges, a spiritual picture making sense and purpose out of previously vague scriptures and the disorder presented to my natural mind and ears.

Merriam-Webster's dictionary defines *idol* essentially as follows:

    1: a representation or symbol of an object of worship, a false god
    2: a likeness of something
    3: a form or appearance visible but without substance
    4: an object of extreme devotion
    5: a false conception

Idolatry was a continual issue with the Israelites, often evoking disfavor and judgment from God. It is difficult to understand why they would so highly revere such obviously impotent objects. Is idolatry a similar problem today? Could we possibly have false gods?

I USED TO do a lot of welding. Welding is an industrial process, which is also an art form. Metal is joined to metal by melting adjoining surfaces and introducing a filler material.

Today most welders wear electronic helmets with a glare shield that is triggered by the flash produced by the electrode to ground arc. The welder can see through the lens which is only slightly tinted until the arc is struck, at which time the lens immediately turns sufficiently dark to shield the welder's eyes from the high-intensity light. Some welders still use helmets without the self-darkening lens. The welder positions his electrode with the helmet raised, so he can see. Just prior to striking the arc, he gives a quick nod of his head, flipping the helmet into position to shield his eyes. While welding, he can see only the small area illuminated by the intense light of the arc.

Accidentally catching the flash of an arc without proper eye protection can be very painful. The pain, not felt immediately, usually increases over a few hours. Having been inadvertently exposed to an arc flash is not always evident. Visitors to a welding shop may unknowingly stare at an arc from a distance, unaware that they are being burned.

Consider God and the welding arc. God mercifully shields us from too much exposure, which would mean terrible pain or even death. Pain or death? But we are consistently taught that exposure to God is a wonderful experience. Wonderful? Long ago, I read that encounters with God produced a different emotion. Here are a few.

> And he was afraid and said, "How awesome is this place!" (Genesis 28:17)

> Therefore, I would be dismayed at His presence; When I consider, I am terrified of Him. (Job 23:15)

> So he came near to where I was standing, and when he came I was frightened and fell on my face. (Daniel 8:17)

> And an angel of the Lord suddenly stood before them, and the glory of the Lord shone around them; and they were terribly frightened. (Luke 2:9–10)

> And when the disciples saw Him walking on the sea, they were frightened, saying, "It is a ghost!" (Matthew 14:26)

> And Zacharias was troubled when he saw him, and fear gripped him. (Luke 1:12)

> And Moses shook with fear. (Acts 7:32)

ONE OF MY first encounters with God was so terrifying that I had no idea what to make of it. I kept that experience and others mostly to myself for years. After mentioning some of my experiences a few times and listening to the questionable responses, I gradually decided to keep quiet.

Though I certainly had pleasant experiences with Him, many were disconcerting and uncomfortable. One time I actually rebuked the voice speaking to me. The words seemed all wrong. "I rebuke You in the Name of Jesus," I said to Jesus. I still have to laugh just thinking about it. Certainly God was amused. Who wouldn't be? He went on to say a lot of things, all of which I initially rejected as being from the Enemy. I simply did not want to hear such things. Over time I came to realize that it was God speaking to me.

GOD SOMETIMES EXPOSES us to more of Him than we can stand, and the exposure can be painful. Like exposure to a welding arc, the pain or damage may not be initially evident. However, once so exposed, the "damage" is done, and we are never the same.

Most people, many people, I don't really know, get just enough of God to barely see what they are doing. Like a large group of welders, welding their discrete lives together behind the safety of vision-protecting helmets, God is perceived as being confined to a small area joining things, performing nicely, and He is likable. He is a good God. But if the blinding helmets are removed and the area surveyed, a stray flash may be caught. God may be seen in a new and unexpected light.

I recall several times failing to get my helmet into place after striking an arc. Seeing a welding arc a few inches from your face is extraordinarily dazzling. The arc is a brilliant, white ball with spikes sticking out all around—very nasty looking. Following is the momentary partial blindness caused by the negative dark arc image, and later the pain of the resulting burn emerges.

Magnify a welding arc up a few trillion times into the flash caused by a nuclear detonation; extrapolate that to infinity, and you have God. I can't even imagine being exposed to a nuclear detonation, much less God, without protection. We know that Moses was exposed to some of God, and the results were visible long afterward. There is apparently coming a time when we shall see God directly and literally stand in His presence without protection. It is impossible for me to truly visualize a positional relationship such as *standing in the presence* of God. God is far more than our loving Father, though He is all of that. God is infinite, dazzling, brilliance beyond comprehension, dangerous, unpredictable, scary and awesome. If being before Him seems easily comprehensible, perhaps some rethinking of who He is may be in order.

I believe that God has exposed us to just a small amount of Himself, but many think they have a much larger part of the picture and offer us a sort of soup. The soup is a mixture of solid Biblical concepts and sound inspiration with varying amounts of man's ideas thrown in to fill in the gaps.

We should guard against adding "filler" and any tendency toward presumption.

A TALE ABOUT some guys who liked to rescue people is occasionally presented at Christian gatherings in various amounts of detail. I've heard this story several times but do not know the source.

The guys, camped out on the beach, used a little boat to help or to rescue people. The locals began to realize that this was a noble effort and decided to erect a little building to shelter the rescuers. The boat guys appreciated the shelter, and all was well. After some time, some of the locals thought that the shelter could be used for some other things, like bake sales, dances, and meetings, which had nothing to do with rescuing people.

As time went on, the shelter was made more elaborate. The boat guys became less well known and their purpose questioned. "Who is this ragtag crew with such a small craft? We need a yacht." Eventually there was no longer room for the boat. So the rescuers moved on down the beach a ways and continued happily rescuing. The locals there appreciated their work and decided to build a shelter. As time went on, the shelter became more elaborate, the guys moved again, and so on.

Thinking about the process of pruning reminds me of the story about the rescuers. Though the same nutrients feed both the stalk and the fruit, if the stalk is allowed to grow continuously, the tree may become unmanageable. Though there may be fruit, it may be inaccessible, of poor quality or low in quantity. Pruning increases fruit yield. With less stalk to feed, the abundance of nutrients produced from the mature root system enhances the fruit yield. Some fruit trees are raised simply for their ornamental value, which is fine, if that's all that is desired. But the purpose of the domesticated, working fruit tree is to bear fruit, accessible fruit—not stalk

What is the true purpose of our lives? Is our Christianity to be merely ornamental, or is it to be fruit bearing? Have the rescuers in our churches moved on down the beach? Did we have any to start with? Are churches and our Christianity functional or just for show?

Fruit can be defined as the result of an action or labor. We are supposed to bear fruit for God; fruit which lasts. The Holy Spirit works in us to bear fruit, nine types of which are listed in Galatians. What is the fruit that we are supposed to produce? Are we producing fruit, mature individuals in whom Christ is plainly evident? Are we able to identify our true spiritual relatives by their fruit, by our unity with them in faith? Or are we more likely to be comfortable with those having similar stalk or ornamentation?

ORNAMENTAL CHRISTIANITY IS pretty common. One can easily recognize it by the abundance of stalk and lack of fruit. The obvious assumption is that I'm talking about traditional brick-and-mortar mainline denominational churches that have only tradition left to their credit. But stalk and ornamentation can be less obvious and much more sinister, infecting the lives and assemblies of those who honestly believe that they are on the cutting edge of God's present-day work. It is the ornamentation of pride over past accomplishments and the stalk of programs, facilities and numbers.

The stalk is a structure upon which fruit is supposed to grow. It is both useful and necessary. There is nothing inherently evil or corrupt about the structure. In fact, little, if anything, that God created is inherently evil or corrupt. It is the application or use that allows an entrance for corruption.

For the rescuers, the shelter was a fine place to keep the boat, but it served a different purpose once they left. The latter inhabitants may have wanted to identify with the rescuers. They may have shown movies of past rescues, and even taught classes on how to conduct rescues, but everybody knew that there was no real rescuing going on. Or did they? Joining in later, merely identifying with the original rescuers can be comforting. To simply be part of such a renowned group can, in itself, be satisfying. Many pastors assure us that just tithing is sufficient to be a participant in producing fruit for the Lord. I don't doubt that giving money is part of the effort, but does that make us, as individuals, truly fruit-bearing?

The existence of a structure can give the illusion of Christian life, but the absence of fruit tells the real story. We want to be viewed as fruit bearing, so we adorn ourselves with the ornamentation of boasting about accomplishments, the ornamentation of degrees, and the stalk of ministries and programs. But God wants actual fruit, and we can't fake that. It doesn't matter how glorious the structure is, if there isn't any fruit.

I once heard a pastor talking about how much he wanted to see God's will being done in his church and he asked everyone who agreed to raise their hands. Of course, just about everyone did. He went on and on about how God had been there time and again during the difficult years of church building, and how he believed that what we were seeing, the beautiful building, the wonderfully groovy worship band, the elaborate sound system and the abundance of facilities was surely a result of his following the Lord every step of the way. I believe it. No doubt. God was in it all the way.

But then I thought, why ask us a question with such an obvious answer? Nobody with a brain would answer in the negative. And why go to such extraordinary lengths to assure us that God had been with this pastor in the past? It's like someone who wants to assure us that they believe in exercise showing us their expensive equipment or a membership in a gym. If the results are obvious, there is no need for assurances, since such explanations are often simple attempts to convince others that what they are seeing is not reality.

If the pastor really wanted God's will to be done, why tell us? Tell God. Tell Him that, *no matter what it costs, let Your will be done.* Then let the results speak for themselves. If you're overweight and out of shape, no amount of telling people that you believe in exercise or eating right will convince anyone that you are anything but a liar. No amount of rehashing past accomplishments, books written, people saved or healed will suffice for a lack of fruit.

God is strangely interested in fruit. He seems to want it in season, every season, and in quantity.

CREDIBILITY AND RESPECT are highly valued in our society and both are pursued. Credibility and respect can have monetary value. We attempt to add credibility to our words by qualifying ourselves before we speak. If we are credible, people respect what we say, even pay for our advice. We place our level of education behind our names, list written books, place certifications on office walls, and properly preface statements. Who really cares? Millions are pouring their thoughts out to us from all directions. In order to get us to listen, they spend precious time listing past accomplishments. Of course, if we are at a business conference or interviewing for a business position, we should pay more attention to someone with relevant experience or credentials.

But church isn't about business, or is it? Speaking for God requires no credentials, and we want to hear from God, don't we? Isn't that the point of listening to a Christian speaker?

Better to let our words stand *on their own*. If we feel we have some wisdom to offer, let God weight the words. He did for Jesus. He can do the same for us. How refreshing it would be to let God do the exalting, for isn't that what we're doing, exalting ourselves, by qualifying ourselves, by stating some reason why our particular advice should be preferred?

How exciting it might be to let God weight our words by His Spirit. We could do that by simply speaking what we believe He has given us to say in quiet confidence. There is no need to shout or add feigned emotion. If the words have weight, it is because He has weighted them. If not, that's okay. Let the words take their place among the other words spoken by mere humans. Let the words from God stand boldly out from the wisdom of mortal man, differentiated only by Him.

There is certainly a place for credentials and diversions. Loud instruments, shouting, singing and all kinds of noise are totally appropriate in worship and celebration of our Creator. But they *alone* are insufficient. They are not a substitute for true obedience and devotion. God plainly tired of the Israelites' empty celebrations.

Adding *unnecessary* effects to church meetings *can* be counter-productive. I have no doubt that God is often present amidst the distracting multimedia displays, hyped qualifications, emotion-drawing drama and world-class music. But where is the *real* focus? There exists the danger that emotion, talent, and entertainment might become more desirable than Him. Just because we *feel* good, does that mean we have truly been in His presence?

Is God alone not sufficient? We should know He is. The real danger is that He might not be in our assemblies. What would we have?

Silence? Good. He might address us as we sit in our uncomfortable silence.

I enjoy entertainment. I need entertainment. All of us do. There is a place for healthy entertainment and, in addition, our assemblies should be open and accessible to everyone, but not necessarily comfortable.

This is difficult, but I cannot shy away from commenting. Healthy dialogue would be welcome. Our assemblies are supposed to be about God. Do we know the difference?

I HAVE PRESENTED the above concepts to introduce a simple sentence that was presented to me. It was late in the winter of 2004, I believe, and I was lying on my back in bed in the middle of the night. The words seemed to appear out of the center of my bedroom ceiling.

"When they come out of her and make a vow of chastity, then the anointings will begin."

I remember the words as being chrome plated in the form of a lightning bolt. I'm not sure if I added the chrome later, but it seems to be associated with the words as I remember them. I rolled over in bed rejecting the words as nothing but nonsense. First of all, I wasn't into chastity. I planned on remarrying and tried my best to ignore anything implying an absence of sex. Also, I had no idea of who *her* was referring to, and it seemed to have little to do with me.

It was around this same time that I began to realize that much of what God had spoken to me about related to the church and had little to do directly with me. But I was not fully aware of that until a friend mentioned it later and more of what I have heard began to make real sense.

After a few weeks, since the words were still on my mind, I ran them by the people attending a group meeting in my home. Home groups are significant. Though the groups can sometimes serve vain purposes, they are ideal vehicles for people to express thoughts and opinions regarding literally anything. In a closed, hopefully secure and safe setting, the personal interaction between believers can open doors long closed because of pain and trauma. I attended many home meetings.

I presented the words to our group of probably ten or so, and the response was mixed. Most agreed that the words were obviously from God and must have some significant meaning. I had some concerns about this. Are we so desperate to hear something from the Lord that we will accept anything coming from a supposedly reliable source? Throwing a piece of questionable meat to hungry people can be dangerous. Sometimes they'll eat anything.

Caution—every word should be judged by itself, not by the package. This time, I believed the words were from God, and some elaboration will be presented below.

FIRST, THOUGH OCCASIONAL surprises are nice, most of us prefer things that come in familiar packages. If the package is good, then we assume that the contents are probably good. Jesus was a strange package to put God in. Just about everybody missed the contents, because the package was so unfamiliar. Wouldn't it make sense that God, wanting us to learn to discern His voice, would possibly package His words in an unfamiliar or even unacceptable way? I can almost hear Him saying, *"Don't look at the package. Learn to hear Me speaking to you. The package is not the point. I keep changing the package so you will not make an idol of it."*

An idol? Would we make idols out of mere packages, like churches, ministries, ministers and books? Would we actually reject His voice in favor of something more pleasant, more familiar?

Consider a verse of scripture.

> But to what shall I compare this generation? It is like children sitting in the marketplaces who call out to the other children and say, "We played the flute for you, and you did not dance; we sang a dirge, and you did not mourn." For John came neither eating nor drinking, and they say, "He has a demon!" The Son of Man came eating and drinking, and they say, "Behold, a gluttonous man and a drunkard, a friend of tax-gatherers and sinners!" Yet wisdom is vindicated by her deeds. (Matthew 11:16–19)

This verse relates to packages and contents. Jesus indicates the difference in packages and the judgments made. He then finishes by saying that the deeds, which imply fruit, since fruit is the result of labor, make good sense or sound action justified. Regardless of the package, the contents are what counts. Regardless of the action, the results are what counts. Have our senses been trained to discern contents and results rather than mere packaging?

OUR GROUP HAD a lengthy discussion regarding the words, *"When they come out of her and make a vow of chastity, then the anointings will begin."* I wish I had the wisdom and clear thinking that was displayed recorded in detail. All I can offer is a condensed version, as well as I can remember it.

I asked, "Is this from God?"

"Well, nobody stands to benefit from the words. There is no reason for you to just think this up. The words relate to several things. You didn't think they were from God at first?"

"I didn't, because of the content. The words *vow* and *chastity* were not words I wanted to hear, I guess."

"Maybe they mean nothing. Maybe he was dreaming. They could be just nonsense."

"You weren't dreaming?"

"No, definitely not."

"I don't think they are nonsense. They sound like something that God would say. Let's take the phrase apart. Vows are mentioned. Somebody have a dictionary?"

"But aren't we told not to make vows? Doesn't the Bible say that?"

"In Acts, Paul and four others apparently made vows. We are told not to make an oath, which is a declaration that our words are true as witnessed by God. We are instructed to let our yes and no be sufficient."

"What about chastity?"

"Yeah. Why would God eliminate sex?"

"That makes little sense."

"Perhaps He wants spiritual purity. Chastity also implies personal integrity, according to my dictionary."

"That would be consistent with the Lord."

"Okay, but what are anointings?"

"Anointings could refer to the appearance of signs and wonders being performed."

"Some of that happens now. Is this a new thing? That's not really new. Maybe they will be on a much higher level or be much more frequent."

"Anointing also refers to election or separating out for special purpose. A special group?"

"Divine election?"

"Possibly, but we're talking about some divisive teachings now. Remember the 'Sons of God' from the seventies or eighties?"

"Let's concentrate on what we have here right now, just these words."

"Okay, but who is *her*?"

"Well, we all know the connotation referred to in Revelation, but this is now. Is there a *her* now that God is concerned about?"

"Jonathan, don't you have any more information on this? Is that all that He said regarding these words?"

"That's it. I'm just the messenger here. I can offer my opinion as to who I think *her* is, but I can't say that opinion is not influenced by my own experience."

"Give us your opinion. Who do *you* think *her* is relating to?"

"I believe that *her* is the existing structure of authority as presumed by any man-made institution of church, any system of so-called coverings and man-elected authority that claims to speak for or represent God. *Her* is church in the form of an idol, a harlot."

There are responsible, selfless pastors and leaders of excellent local churches dedicated to pursuing the work of the Lord. Such leaders and churches deserve our attendance and support. Perfection is not expected or possible. In fact, chaos and disorganization may be more obvious where true work is being done.

There are churches that require members to submit to its leadership's authority. Though we should properly submit one to another and to those in proper authority around us, true authority comes only from God. If a church becomes an authority in itself, placing people in positions of authority by its own authority to serve its own purposes, then the church is not worthy of our submission or obedience. If the ministry or church becomes a purpose of itself, like a politician whose true desire is to preserve his office, we should not submit to or support such an institution. We should remain in opposition to and come out of such a place. Jesus did not submit to authority which opposed God's. Simply being under some religious authority is not a substitute for God's authority.

Careful consideration of the definition of an idol may bring to light some misplaced priorities in our own lives. Consider especially that an idol is a *form or appearance visible but without substance* and/or a *false conception.*

> For men will be ... lovers of pleasure rather than lovers of God; holding to a form of godliness, although they have denied its power. (2 Timothy 3:4–5)

If there is the possibility that church, church life, people or ministries have been idolized, what else could be turned into an idol by attributing to it near deity status?

EARLY IN MY Christian life, Art once asked me to accompany him to his basement for a serious discussion. Art was the one who later sat with me during the anxiety attacks I experienced after my first wife, Cathie, left. We went down to his basement and sat together on two old stuffed recliners. It appeared to me that he intended to share a secret conversation and did not want anything overheard. He looked around as if to assure himself that we hadn't been followed and that no listening devices had been positioned in some remote corner of the room.

"I wanted to come down here," he said, "to ask you a question that can get you into trouble merely by asking it."

Cool, I thought to myself. I like this. Here is a man who has been a pastor, headed fellowships, married and buried, raised children, and has obviously been a servant of God, confiding in me. I'm honored. The question must be of grave importance.

He held up his worn and frayed Bible for my examination and asked, "What do you think of this?"

"Your Bible?"

"Yes."

I was puzzled. "What? What about it?"

"Do you think that this *is* the *Word of God* or that it *contains* the *word of God*?"

Now I was the one looking around for dangerous listening devices. Should I play it safe and lie, or should I tell him my true thoughts and invite more trouble? Trouble and disagreement were not, and still are not, hard to find. It seems there is usually something to argue about when knowledge is held in such high esteem.

I told Art where I stood.

IT *CAN* BE misleading, confusing and possibly idolatrous to refer to the Bible as the *Word of God*. Though many, including myself, often refer to the Bible as *the word*, Jesus is the true *Word of God*. The following observations are not intended to be a criticism of the Bible, but a simple warning about elevating the Bible to the position of an idol. Big difference.

Art asked me a valid question and, though I was much less acquainted with the Bible at that time, my basic answer was the same then as it is now; I prefer to say the Bible *contains* the *word of God*. I maintain that preference out of simple deference to Jesus and to the prophets who have brought the *word of the Lord* to darkened generations. Others prefer to call the Bible the *Word of God* or the *word of God*. My concern is not about that preference. It is about idolatry.

Jesus is priceless. Words from God are priceless. Both should stand out like jewels in mud and clay, like beacons on a stormy sea from words of mere humans. Jesus brought life to us. Words straight from God continue to bring vitality and life to sustain us in a world which seems to grow only darker.

There are many words in the Bible that are not words from God. I have heard sermons based on words *written* in the Bible, but attributed to obviously questionable people. For example, the following statements are in the Bible:

> But the Pharisees were saying, "He casts out the demons by the ruler of the demons." (Matthew 9:34)

The man answered and said to them, "Well, here is an amazing thing that you do not know where He is from, and yet He opened my eyes. We know that God does not hear sinners; but if anyone is God-fearing, and does His will, He hears him." (John 9:30–31)

And when they had summoned them, they commanded them not to speak or teach at all in the name of Jesus. (Acts 4:18)

The above words are all written in the Bible, and they are references to the words of heathen. The first statement is definitely not true. The second is a source of debate. The third is an admonishment to refrain from something we are certainly supposed to do. God did not say any of these things. There are numerous other examples.

Words spoken by prophets are referred to as *the word of the Lord* in the Bible, which is appropriate. The *word of God* or *word of the Lord* is plainly recorded in many places, so it is obvious that the Bible *at least contains* the *word of God.*

Though the Bible be inerrant, inspired by God, without equal, and the greatest book ever written, it is still a shadow of God. We serve the living God, the very definition of life, not the Bible. To defend their doctrines against external criticism, some have deified the Bible, making it off-limits for criticism or questioning in any way.

Our faith is not supposed to be in the Bible, it is supposed to be in Jesus. We do not pray to the Bible, worship the Bible, nor is the Bible some supernatural object. Though certain numbers have meaning and some versions may be technically more accurate, we should disregard fascinations with superstitious attributes like secret codes, numerology or a particular version's being somehow divinely correct over another.

The Bible is subject to interpretation by mortals, who make mistakes. Those interpretations cause conflict and divisions. The mere existence of hundreds of denominations having conflicting interpretations of basic Bible passages is simple evidence that opinions vary. The often-made claim that the Bible is self-interpreting is meaningless. By definition, the act of interpretation requires an intermediary or rephrasing to enhance comprehension. Mistakes are unavoidable regardless of claims suggesting infallibility. How can there be a "correct" interpretation of scripture when each interpreter grades his own paper?

Though God has spoken to me of things not directly presented in the Bible, nothing has conflicted with what I have found in the Bible. Some of what He has said initially seemed to contradict what I believed to be sound doctrine, but He patiently endured my doubts and complaints. Over time, He provided conclusive proof through additional inspiration, instruction from others or personal experience to convince at least me that He has been speaking to me and that nothing He has related to me contradicts what I see in scripture. Yet, even as I attempt to relate to others what I believe are His words, I am aware of my personal potential for errors and my sole responsibility for such errors.

The *significant* point is that God spoke to me *first* and my subsequent research confirmed that it was Him. If *too* much emphasis is placed on pure scripture study with only *assumed* guidance from His Spirit, judgments based on carnal understanding are possible, precluding acceptance of anything outside that understanding.

I once heard a pastor asking someone to place themselves under the Bible, under its authority. I would refuse. The request is essentially asking that person to place themselves in obedience to that pastor's interpretation of the Bible. The Bible is not an authority, a code, or a set of rules. It is a testimony.

Challenges to the Bible's authenticity have provoked unnecessary expenditures of energy often exposing us as insecure and defensive. Such challenges will probably continue unabated.

We are not harmed by someone's critique of our doctrinal positions. Our time and energy would be better spent recognizing and seeking ways to reconcile and work with our true spiritual brothers and sisters from any culture. Doctrinal differences should not be a source of disputes. Grace and love should rule.

I do not doubt that God inspired the entire Bible. I have no criticisms of the Bible. There is nothing to criticize. But why risk idolatry by placing any object so close to a level reserved for our Creator alone? The level of deity belongs only to God.

SOME HAVE FASHIONED two golden calves for people to turn to, two idols which can be interpreted, misused, manipulated and worshiped. If church attendance or Biblical knowledge has become our hope, our confidence, a substitution for God, one or both have become idols. If we defend either as infallible and above criticism, they are idols. God, who truly is infallible and above criticism, does not even defend Himself.

Neither the Bible nor church is an idol of itself. Idols are made of objects by attributing to them deity status. Only God is worthy of our worship, of the status of deity, and we should have no other gods before Him.

14

Transition

Grace to you and peace from God our Father, and the Lord Jesus Christ, who gave Himself for our sins, that He might deliver us out of this present evil age ... (Gal 1:3-4)

TRANSITION CAN BE difficult. Doctors tell us that the transition from the womb to the world is traumatic for a newborn. Teens find themselves entering adult life piecemeal; emotions, hormones, physical characteristics, perceptions and understanding commonly arrive at different times. The process is almost like ordering a complex machine and having it arrive one component at a time. Until the whole thing is put together properly, it might only take up space or could even be dangerous. The muscle cars of the sixties and seventies remind me of teenagers. Big motors were introduced before the development of good brakes.

> As a sidebar, I owned a 1968 Shelby GT500. Very fast. I recall being quite pleased as the speedometer quickly passed 120. But, suddenly realizing that a stop sign was not far ahead, I stood on the brakes. Though the brakes were sufficient to *eventually* stop the car, they got so hot that the interior filled with smoke. We had to evacuate the thing and I was concerned that the car itself might catch on fire. I traded for a '66 Corvette with disk brakes on all four wheels. It stopped quickly—a better deal.

Life in transition can be chaotic. Viewed externally, transition appears sometimes messy, disorganized and, most importantly, out of control. Control is the main issue. A psychiatrist friend once told me that the first thing he tries to determine about his patient is the patient's opinion regarding who or what is controlling the events of their lives. Perceived or real, loss of control usually causes fear, anxiety and depression. Paul wrote in the book of Acts, "Through many tribulations we must enter the kingdom of God." The fear and anxiety many have felt from real loss of control over the events of their lives seems possible as the transition from personal-control to true God-control progresses. That transition can be dramatic and traumatic.

The kingdom of God is the realm in which God is king. Jesus claimed that the kingdom of God was among those He was among, and that the kingdom was *at hand.* Being at hand implies that something is currently available. The kingdom of God is currently available to us, but we need to do more than learn about it, talk about it, and be entertained by music and sermons alluding to it. We need to actually enter.

Affection for, knowledge of, and worship of God is not sufficient. Too many have an affection for the Lord, but do not do what He says. Affection or emotional feelings for Him may come and go. We are commanded to love Him, and He says that to love Him is to obey Him. We must come under His authority and control. Paul clearly implies that entrance is gained through tribulation, pressure and trials. I disagree with the assumption that entrance, true entrance, can be gained any other way.

Entrance into the kingdom of God is a transition from a life under our control to a life under the control of God. In the past I avoided using the word *control* regarding God's authority in our lives because, to some, a lack of accountability on our part or too much intrusion on God's part may be inferred. I was more comfortable with terms like *rule by consent* or *submission to God.* There are other terms, like *permissive will,* that are commonly used to imply a looser relationship between what might please God and what might actually take place. To dwell on these distinctions is to miss a more important aspect of God's divine intervention in our lives. Whether we drive a Ford or a Chevy, or live on the north or south end of town can be irrelevant to God's particular plan, which I've referred to as our destiny. Not everything impacts our destiny, and there is a certain irrelevance regarding what pleases God.

What did Jesus mean when He implied that He did nothing but

that which He saw His father doing? He certainly made a distinction between mundane events, which He did not need to see the Father doing, and destiny-determining events, actions relating to His purpose. So should we. Though God is aware of and concerned about the details of our lives, He is pleased that we take responsibility for not only the mundane details of our lives, but also for what affects our destiny. Sharing with us must bring pleasure to Him and we have a definite responsibility for good stewardship of that with which we have been entrusted.

We are not robots, mere automatons waiting for the next signal to move in a particular direction.

I HAVE USED the term *fix* to indicate a process of healing or restoration of some sort, which results in a paradox. Several friends seemed to be convinced that I needed some internal adjustment, which, once accomplished, would end my discomfort. Even better, it would make me available to God for some productive use. I saw them picturing me as a device having a loose connection, causing some interruption or scrambling of the communication between God and me. The occasional grounding and sparking of that loose wire often caused others some discomfort. Since some people could apparently not get through to me, it was assumed that God could not either. The implication was, of course, that I was of little use as I was. One person actually said so directly.

Divorcees, depression sufferers, singles, and others similarly broken and not conforming to the married-with-job-and-kids standard, are commonly rejected for positions of church responsibility. Perhaps such people are considered unreliable and may short-circuit at a critical time, which might be unpleasant. Could it be possible that God might actually want, or honestly prefer, to use some people in a need-of-repair state? If so, why is there such emphasis on and so much written about *fixing* people? Might a new, deeper understanding of the term *broken* be in order? The paradox is that by fixing what appears to be broken, we may render the thing, the person, less useful.

God uses broken people.

ONE MAN ASKED me once how God could know everything. I explained that if God is omniscient, He knows all information, past, present and future. He knows the minute details of our lives; and nothing, absolutely nothing, escapes His awareness. I referred earlier to an incident which happened years ago. A person concluded that I had gotten myself into a place where God could not help me. It had to do with my confession. If God is omnipotent, nothing is beyond His ability to control; yes, even our will. For example, he can and does bend the will of others to show us favor. Though there may be some validity to an argument that He honors our free choice, He certainly allows much into our lives which is against our personal will or pleasure.

If He is omnipresent, He is everywhere. No one can hide from Him or be beyond His reach. If it were otherwise, think about this. How could we totally and without reservation commit ourselves, our entire being, into His care? If he were not able to control every event in the universe, then something random could happen to us. That cannot be. Our lives are truly wholly in His capable hands.

No. He runs everything, does not deny His responsibility and, I believe, is delighted to share that responsibility with mere mortals. As many stumble around trying to carve out the boundaries of their relationship with Him, defining and therefore limiting Him, setting any standard other than Him and His voice, He watches; trying, testing, refining and allowing the sifting and sorting to continue. For many are called, but few are chosen.

ENTRANCE INTO THE kingdom of God is a transition from our control to His control. We may be allowed to exercise autonomy or authority to various degrees; but, rest assured, He watches everything. Nothing happens to us that He does not allow, regulate, or make provision for.

Jesus is Lord of all. Why serve a lesser god?

15

Help is Huge

If help is hard to find, maybe you're not looking
around enough.

THE CONTEXT OF the events and dialogues I've described would
be incomplete without an acknowledgment of the help that I have
received. Though God's offerings have been meager at times by my standards,
sometimes humbling, often barely ahead of a deadline and have frequently
come from unlikely sources, He has helped me all the way. I can hardly
think of a thing that I have accomplished without help of some kind. Not
that I have accomplished a lot. My point is not to measure my successes and
failures, but to reveal a significant method He has used to indicate to me
where I am positioned in reference to my walk on His narrow road to my
destiny.

I can recall many lively discussions about how to determine God's
will. Few of them began by actually defining *will*. If someone were to ask
me to look for something unfamiliar, first a description of the thing would
be helpful.

"What are you trying to find?"
"God's will."
"What exactly is that?"
"I think it's what He wants to be done."
"Like a certain choice among several possibilities?"
"Could be, but I'm not sure of what's possible or what's on His mind."
"How will you know if you've found it?"
"I'll have peace, or things will work out, or I'll feel better."
"So, if you're comfortable, you've found it?"
"Right."

Wrong. Though *comfort* is a word frequently found in the Bible, *comfortable* is not in any of mine. Nor is there any indication that we should expect things to work out in our lives, or that we should be free from stress.

To do someone's will is to do their pleasure or desire. It has already been mentioned that God's pleasure or desire is not necessarily a succession of events, nor necessarily even related to a succession of events. Certainly our worship of Him, our trust of Him, and our attitude of gratefulness, though no doubt His desire, are not truly related to any actual event sequence. Each one of us must establish our own relationship with our Lord. It is unwise to attempt to pattern our relationships with anyone, much less our relationship with God, after another's. Biblical verses about imitation refer to faith, or some quality of spirituality or virtue. Even Jesus instructed His disciples to avoid clinging too much to His fleshly incarnation. He desired that they pursue a relationship of true spiritual nature, not one based on any imitation of Him.

Although I do not have a key to determine what specific action places anyone within the confines of God's pleasure, I can hardly recall struggling significantly to determine what His will was. Yet the question turns up regularly from sincere believers. Whether certain of my personal choices have been anywhere near God's will has been questioned so often since I became involved with Him that I try to avoid discussing it anymore. It isn't possible to give a reasonable answer to a question when the question itself is not defined or is presented as condemnation or an accusation.

I'M NOT SURE exactly what purpose God had in mind in asking me to write down my experiences with Him. Personally, I hope to shed some light on alternate possibilities for being in the right place with the Lord. The shear guilt and confusion experienced by people who are being tried or tested by God is bad enough without being magnified by inconsiderate and religious-minded well-doers who are certain some sin or error surely must be present in the sufferer.

If these words appear harsh, perhaps it may be time for some harshness and bottom-lining, a time for getting back to some basics in evaluating just what our Christianity is about and what God truly finds pleasing.

THOUGH I'VE STRUGGLED immensely with God throughout the past five years, He has reminded me of His determination to complete His work. The next dialogue occurred over a period of time. The words gradually formed in my mind in the winter of 2005–2006, during the dismal days of trudging from one company to another as the rain poured down in Portland and Seattle. I complained bitterly about the senselessness of the ordeal and the lack of results. God's response, which is a Biblically common response, was to pose a question.

The question seemed odd. Was it really God or my own thoughts? It took months for the words to form clearly, and for me to respond coherently.

> *"Do you want me to save you or not?"*
> "Save me?"
> *"Do you want me to save you or not?"*
> "Now?"
> *"Do you?"*
> "Do I want you to save me?"
> *"Do you want me to save you or not, Jonathan?"* He had to repeat the phrase many, many times until I grasped His point. Was God really asking a question with such an *obvious* answer? Why? It was difficult to believe He would actually ask me such a thing. If God would not ask a superfluous question, maybe the answer wasn't so obvious.
> "Yes, Lord, I want you to save me."
> *"I'm doing that."*

Doing that? Could saving someone actually be *so difficult*? Was I some extraordinarily obstinate case, a case which required such extreme measures to arrive at a result, a result which seemed so simple for others? A scripture fell into my brain.

> For it is time for judgment to begin with the household of God; and if it begins with us first, what will be the outcome for those who do not obey the gospel of God? And if it is with difficulty that the righteous is saved, what will become of the godless man and the sinner? Therefore, let those also who suffer according to the will of God entrust their souls to a faithful Creator in doing what is right. (1 Peter 4:17–19)

As I knelt by my bed to pray, He said, *"This is not a game, Jonathan. This is life and death. Do not lightly regard my chastening. This is serious. This is life and death."*

"Blah, blah … suffering … blah, blah," some Sunday morning teacher droned on a few years back.

"Excuse me, uh," I said, slightly waving my raised hand.

"Yes? You have a question?"

"Yeah. How do we suffer?"

"Excuse me?"

"Suffer. How do we suffer?" I repeated.

"Well, by being persecuted," the teacher said confidently. What could be so obvious?

"Persecuted? How are we, here in the United States, suffering under persecution?"

"Well, we may lose our jobs or something for being a Christian."

"Have you?"

"What?"

"Ever lost a job, or know anyone who lost a job because they were a Christian?"

"No, not exactly."

"So how have you, or anyone you know, been persecuted?"

"Well, we're really going beyond the lesson here. But that is a good question," he admitted. We moved on, maybe. I don't remember.

TO CLAIM THAT we, in this wonderful Christian-based United States, suffer persecution is to do grave injustice to those who suffer true persecution for their Christian faith in other countries. Certainly there may be isolated incidents of persecution, but they are rare in this country. If persecution is so rare, how then do we suffer? Job's famous suffering was not persecution for his faith. He suffered by losing stuff, by being insulted, accused and misunderstood.

Various Bible verses make it clear that there is suffering that is experienced according to the will of God and suffering which results from our own errors. Though we clearly all sin, not all suffering is related to committed sins. That is, suffering may not be the consequence of sin by us or anyone else. Jesus made that clear in the example of the man born blind in John 9:2. Also, people can suffer even though they are doing what is right. 1 Peter 2:20–21 says, "But if when you do what is right and suffer for it, you patiently endure, this finds favor with God." And it is ludicrous to call the devastation resulting from extreme weather a direct consequence of the sins of the individuals affected. If we suffer, it is important to attempt to determine the cause.

Though God's principles hold true, formulae, standard procedures for producing results in our spiritual lives, are based on false assumptions. God deals with us individually. I've presented my personal experiences regarding His guidance and instruction. Others have had different experiences. Deterioration and loss in my life have resulted both from the consequences of sin and from trials ordained by God. Discernment, honest self-examination, careful consideration of the opinions of trusted friends, openness and honesty before God have always ultimately revealed to me the nature of the problems. God has no reason to hide from anyone the cause of suffering which results from the consequences of sin. Honest soul-searching, through prayer and listening to others, should reveal any error, though the one committing the sin may remain in denial. In such cases the consequences may continue indefinitely.

As true Christians, if we are suffering and it is not due to the consequences of sin, then it is according to the will of God. If it is according to the will of God, the suffering must be allowed to run its course. There is nothing which should, nor can be done to remedy the situation, and meddling may only extend the ordeal. Certainly, supplications for protection or relief should be continued.

I've made no attempt to hide the fact that I consider the experiences of these last five years to contain suffering according to the will of God. I also am not attempting to quantify or qualify the pain I have experienced. I have no idea how my pain compares to the pain of others. Suffering is painful. It actually hurts sometimes almost unbearably. That's why it is called suffering. But I *have* tried to reveal some of the poor attitude, lack of social skills and bad behavior that I've exhibited.

I would prefer to be regarded as contemptuous in some way that the grace of God might be more valued. I am honored to stand with, to be identified with those who have been misunderstood, experienced rejection and may feel remorse over their poor responses to others who react inappropriately to their situations. All must be forgiven. That's understood. But that the Lord would continue, seemingly unfazed by my complaints and emotional exhibitions, to treat me as a son, that He would continue to teach me and provide for me, is a tribute only to Him and to His amazing grace.

Though sin and wrong choices may be a significant cause of my pain, I have concluded that the primary purpose for my suffering has been for chastening, according to the will of God, and goes beyond the consequences of blatant sin. I know this, because I know that I am on the narrow road to my destiny. One reason that I know that I am on that road is because the help is always there. Help is huge.

THOUGH MY PREVIOUSLY ordered existence has been reduced to living like a sort of vagabond, it is not hard to see His provision and purpose each step of the way. In fact, His provision and purpose have always been the determining factors in discerning His will. Though purpose has played a crucial role, much of that purpose will have to remain between Him and me. Here, it is only appropriate to discuss His provision. His larger purpose has been neatly woven into seemingly pointless wanderings in recent years. The journey truly has been one of making up for lost time.

God has never asked me to do something without providing the means. Whether that principle is universal or not, I don't know. I would assume it is, and I've heard teachers claim so. In every business venture, every risky attempt to perform on difficult manufacturing contracts, every desperate move from city to city, new job, new church, in every difficult situation where I have questioned whether God even had a clue as to what He was doing, someone has always shown up to help me. Every time. Period. It isn't that my contributions have been insignificant. I've worked hard, and I bring a lot to the table. That's not the point. The significant point is, I believe that God has been delighted to see a son step out *beyond* traditional bounds believing that He will, if necessary, even rescue him from his own self-assuredness.

Have I made poor choices? Certainly. Have I failed? Many times. Have I displayed contempt, jealousy and self-righteousness? Endlessly. But the combined effect of all of these experiences has been to convince me of one simple fact, that He has been there and helped me all the way—and that His grace is endless. If I needed a business partner, he was there. God apparently knows that I could not nor did I desire to run a business by myself. If I needed fellowship, people showed up. If I needed instruction, instruction was provided. My standard of living has often borne little relation to the quantity or quality of my effort. God has determined how I will live. Whatever I needed, be it counseling, a Bible study, comfort, guidance, money or a shoulder to cry on, all has been mysteriously provided as I was willing to recognize it—or, actually, to recognize Him.

RECOGNITION IS THE key—recognizing Him, His voice, His provision and His purpose. Recognizing, acknowledging, and accepting Him are keys to staying in His will. He may present Himself in all manner of vague or mysterious packages. He may defy everything we know and hold dear. He may ask of us what is difficult or seemingly impossible so that trust can be learned. But once we are trained to follow only His voice, He can take us places we can't even imagine.

Yet if we restrict Him to our imposed limitations, to our accepted standards, acknowledge Him only in what *we* regard as appropriate for Him, we then self-impose a limit on how far we will follow Him. We then retreat to a confined space of false security, a space of our own limitations. Is He then truly our Lord? Is the space that we retreat to our kingdom or His? He may beckon us to cross a line we have drawn between us and some unknown territory. Might that line be the territorial boundary between our domain and His? Can we trust Him sufficiently to cross that line? There will be more to say about such a significant concept at a later time.

I believe that God delights in our stepping up to the plate and beyond, placing ourselves on and over the line, risking *even failure* to experience Him in a deeper way. God is boundless and limitless.

But My righteous one shall live by faith; And if he shrinks back, My soul has no pleasure in him. (Hebrews 10:38)

Epilogue

OKAY, SO THE first and last conversations did not actually take place, but Brad is the type of guy that can be imagined in many dialogues. Venturing with him into fantasy is always worth the trip. Conversing with Brad is, well, enjoyable, and you never know Who might wander in.

"Hey, Jonathan."

"Hey, Brad. What's up?"

"Not much. You still writing?"

"Yep. In fact, this is the epilogue."

"So what happens to me?"

"What do you mean?"

"I mean, you said that I was a composite of a whole bunch of people; that I was just a character in your book. What happens to me?"

"Nothing. You're still there, just as always. I see you every day, brother, every day. You are alive and well."

"That's nice to know. I thought that I would vaporize or something after you stopped writing."

"Not possible, bro. This is just part of your story. You go on and on and on."

"You know, I've learned a lot from you, buddy. You're pretty difficult sometimes, but I listen. It's been good, though I do think you can forget that everybody has pain, perhaps in ways that you don't see."

"Well said, Brad. I'm sure I miss a lot. You know, I've learned a ton from you too. I really have. All these years of conversations and experiences; it has been very rich. Life has been rich. If the richness of life is measured by the quality and quantity of experiences, my life has been abundantly rich. Maybe that's what the Lord means by 'abundant life.'"

"Well, that's nice to hear. Yeah, we've rocked and rolled at times, had a few arguments and some misunderstandings, for sure. I'm not sure that you've gotten it all straight, but I think you're getting it."

"I hear you. I'm listening."

"Your life is going to be satisfying someday, bro."

"You're sure?"

"Sure, I'm sure. You can bank ... hmmm. Well, I'll tell you what."

"What?"

"I'll lay a thousand bucks on the table on that. It's worth that to me."

"You're kidding!"

"I'm not. I want to see good things for you. I do. I love you, man. You're family."

"Well, now. There *You* are again in another strange package."

"What? What strange package? What are you talking about? Am I a strange package?"

"Uh, nothing, Brad. Just thinking out loud. Hey, I was only kidding before. I really didn't expect your money."

"Maybe, and maybe you were just being a little ornery?"

"Yeah, well, maybe."

"Sure. Sure. Anyway, I think you're getting closer, you know?"

"Closer? What do you mean? I know I'm still not there, wherever that is. But what do you mean by closer?"

"Come on, Jonathan, you know."

"What?"

"Eyes, man. I think you're doing better at keeping your eyes on Him. That's what."

"You know what, Brad?"

"What, buddy?"

"I think you're right. I think I see Him more clearly now. In fact, He's kind of standing in front of me right now. Yeah."

"See? You're getting it, bro! He's there all the time. You just got to *see* Him. You're gonna be fine. It's gonna get better for you real soon. I can tell. And the money is there, if you want to go that way."

"Aw, forget the money. Anyway, you might win. Things have to improve sometime." I thought for a moment and said, "Hey, Brad?"

"What?"

"Thanks."

"For what?"

"You know—all the help."

"Anytime, bro. An-ee-time. That's what I'm here for."

"Love you, brother."

"Love you, too."

"See ya."

"You bet. Yep, you bet."

What TIME Tuesday?

By James Tomasi
www.whattimetuesday.com

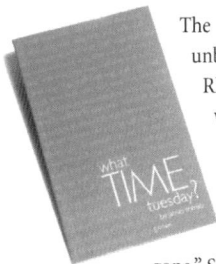

The medical doctors described it as the 'Suicide Disease'. Due to the unbearable pain, I planned how I was going to end my life. My wife Rhonda always pleaded with me to hang on. Now, I wasn't insane: I was just too tired to fight anymore. I chose a Tuesday in February, 1997 to end it all.

On a Friday evening, Rhonda came upstairs. "I am going out for some groceries, honey. Don't do anything stupid while I'm gone." She told me sternly, looking deeply into my eyes. Neither of us knew that her decision to leave me alone that night would change both of our lives forever. A woman on the radio related her experience of Fibromyalgia, asking, "Do you have pain you just can't bear?" Have you been told, "You'll just have to learn to live with it?" She passionately shared knowledge of a scientific technique that had relieved her suffering, thus delivering her from her prison of pain. Rhonda bounded upstairs to share how God had sent the answer. "We're going to an Upper Cervical doctor's office on Tuesday!" The rest of their story and explanations of this unknown science is detailed in their book, *what Time tuesday?* They have dedicated their lives to bringing this knowledge to those suffering or in failing health.

The unbearable pain in my swollen testicle disappeared the day after my UC correction - Daniel C., NV

Gall Bladder now functions and I've had FEWER colds and illnesses - Michelle G

Migraines and pneumonia gone after UC correction - Carolyn F, CA

Rotator cuff pain leaves after an UC correction - Shirley V, CA

15 year-old boy stops bedwetting after 1st correction - KY

Additional testimonials are available at www.whattimetuesday.com

---

To order your copy, call (704) 323-9250 or email us at whattimetuesday@gmail.com

The book is available in MP3 and CD ($5.00) formats, as well as E-book ($3.75) and paper-back copy ($5.00). Quantity discounts are available!

Upper Cervical Advocates & Authors,
James & Rhonda Tomasi

About the Author

Jonathan Bell has been a corporate engineer, a logger, and the co-owner of a machining and fabricating business. Originally from the Baltimore area, Jonathan moved to Idaho in the early '70s. While his travels have taken him in many directions, his love of the Northwest continues to draw him back to the state he calls home. His passions include designing machines, dirt biking, bicycling, playing keyboards, writing, and deep conversations with friends and with God, who has captured his heart. Jonathan lives near Coeur d'Alene, Idaho.

AUTHOR CONTACT INFORMATION

You may contact the author at:
Unbridled Word Works
P.O. Box 1301
Hayden, ID 83835

208-772-5397 **[p]**
jb@unbridledwordworks.com **[e]**

www.unbridledwordworks.com **[I]**

Additional copies of this book are available at

www.unbridledwordworks.com
also available in audio formats-CD or for downloading.

email:

info@unbridledwordworks.com

write:

Unbridled Word Works

P.O. Box 1301

Hayden, ID 83835

call:

208-772-5397

Or please inquire at your local book store

Un*bridled*
WORD WORKS.com